Neuropsychology

Exploring the Complex Connections between Brain Function and Understanding the Science behind Behavior, Cognition, and Emotion

Lewis Finan

Table of Contents

Introduction 8

Chapter 1: Introduction to Neuropsychology 12

1.1 Definition and Scope...14

1.2 Historical Perspectives..16

1.3 Key Theories and Models..19

1.4 Methods and Tools in Neuropsychology 21

Chapter 2: Brain Anatomy and Function 25

2.1 Overview of Brain Structure 27

2.2 Major Brain Regions and Their Functions..29

2.3 Neural Communication: Neurons and Synapses 32

2.4 Neuroplasticity: The Brain's Ability to Change 34

Chapter 3: Cognitive Processes and Brain Function 38

3.1 Attention and Perception 40

3.2 Memory Systems: Short-term and Long-term Memory 43

3.3 Language and Communication 46

3.4 Executive Functions: Planning, Decision-Making, and Problem-Solving 49

Chapter 4: Emotional Processes and Brain Function....................................53

4.1 Understanding Emotions: Theories and Models 56

4.2 The Role of the Limbic System..59

4.3 Emotional Regulation and Dysregulation 63

4.4 The Impact of Stress and Trauma on the Brain 67

Chapter 5: Neuropsychology of Behavior..71

5.1 Motor Functions and Coordination 74

5.2 Behavioral Inhibition and Impulsivity 78

5.3 Social Behavior and Interpersonal Relationships.................................82

5.4 Neurodevelopmental and Behavioral Disorders 85

Chapter 6: Cognitive and Emotional Disorders...89

6.1 Neuropsychological Assessment and Diagnosis 92

6.2 Cognitive Disorders: Dementia, Alzheimer's disease, and Others.......96

6.3 Mood Disorders: Depression, Bipolar Disorder, and Anxiety 100

6.4 Psychotic Disorders: Schizophrenia and Other Psychoses.................104

Chapter 7: Neuropsychological Interventions and Therapies 109

7.1 Rehabilitation Techniques and Strategies 112

7.2 Cognitive Behavioral Therapy (CBT) and Other Therapeutic Approaches 116

7.3 Pharmacological Interventions 120

Chapter 8: Future Directions in Neuropsychology 130

8.1 Advances in Neuroimaging and Brain Mapping..133

8.2 The Role of Genetics and Epigenetics in Neuropsychology 138

8.3 Ethical Considerations in Neuropsychological Research and Practice...............................142

8.4 The Future of Neuropsychology: Integrating Neuroscience, Psychology, and Technology...........146

Conclusion 150

Introduction

Neuropsychology, the study of the intricate connections between brain function and behavior, is a field that continues to expand our understanding of the human experience. At its core, neuropsychology seeks to decipher the complex mechanisms underlying our thoughts, emotions, and actions by examining how the brain operates. This exploration is not just an academic exercise; it holds profound implications for medicine, psychology, education, and everyday life.

Understanding Behavior, Cognition, and Emotion

Behavior, cognition, and emotion are fundamental aspects of what it means to be human. Our behaviors, the actions we take in response to internal and external stimuli, are influenced by a myriad of neurological processes. Cognition encompasses the mental processes involved in gaining knowledge and comprehension, including thinking, knowing, remembering, judging, and problem-solving. Emotion refers to the complex experience of consciousness, bodily sensation, and behavior that reflects the personal significance of an event.

The Brain: A Symphony of Interconnected Systems

The brain is an organ of staggering complexity. Comprising approximately 86 billion neurons, each interconnected in a vast and dynamic network, it orchestrates the functions that define our existence. Neuropsychology dives deep into this symphony of interconnected systems, exploring how different brain regions and networks contribute to distinct cognitive functions and emotional states.

The Evolution of Neuropsychological Science

Historically, the field of neuropsychology has its roots in the early observations of brain-injured patients. Pioneering figures like Paul Broca and Carl Wernicke identified specific brain regions associated with language functions, laying the groundwork for understanding the localization of brain functions. With the advent of modern neuroimaging techniques, such as functional MRI and PET scans, our ability to observe and measure brain activity in real time has exponentially increased, offering unprecedented insights into the living brain.

Neuropsychology in Practice

The applications of neuropsychology are as diverse as they are profound. Clinically, neuropsychologists diagnose and treat conditions ranging from traumatic brain injuries to neurodegenerative diseases like Alzheimer's. In educational settings, they work to understand and support children with learning disabilities. In the realm of mental health, neuropsychological insights inform therapies for conditions such as depression, anxiety, and schizophrenia. Moreover, the principles of neuropsychology are increasingly applied in fields like artificial intelligence and human-computer interaction, where understanding human cognition can lead to the development of smarter, more intuitive technologies.

Bridging the Gap between Science and Experience

This book aims to bridge the gap between scientific research and the lived human experience. By delving into the latest findings in neuropsychology, we will explore how brain function impacts every aspect of our lives, from the mundane to the extraordinary. We will journey through case studies that illuminate the realities of neurological disorders, unravel the mysteries of brain plasticity and cognitive resilience, and consider the ethical implications of emerging neurotechnologies.

A Journey through the Mind

"Neuropsychology: Exploring the Complex Connections between Brain Function and Understanding the Science behind Behavior, Cognition, and Emotion" invites readers to embark on a journey through the mind. Whether you are a student, a professional in the field, or simply a curious reader, this book will provide a comprehensive and engaging exploration of how our brains shape who we are. By understanding the science behind behavior, cognition, and emotion, we can gain deeper insights into ourselves and those around us, ultimately enhancing our ability to navigate the complexities of human life.

Chapter 1: Introduction to Neuropsychology

Neuropsychology, an interdisciplinary field at the intersection of psychology and neuroscience, is dedicated to understanding how the structure and function of the brain relate to specific psychological processes and behaviors. This branch of science delves into the complexities of how our brains shape our thoughts, emotions, and actions, offering profound insights into the human experience.

At its core, neuropsychology aims to unravel the mysteries of brain-behavior relationships. It examines how different areas of the brain contribute to various cognitive functions, such as memory, attention, language, and problem-solving. By studying individuals with brain injuries or neurological disorders, neuropsychologists can identify which regions are responsible for specific functions, thus mapping out the brain's intricate architecture. This field has evolved significantly over the past century, moving from basic observational studies to advanced neuroimaging techniques that allow for real-time observation of brain activity.

Historically, the roots of neuropsychology can be traced back to the work of early pioneers like Paul Broca and Carl Wernicke in the 19th century. Broca's and Wernicke's discoveries about language production and comprehension localized in specific brain regions were foundational, highlighting the concept of functional specialization within the brain. These early findings laid the groundwork for subsequent research and understanding of the brain's organization.

In the modern era, neuropsychology benefits from a variety of sophisticated tools and technologies. Functional magnetic resonance imaging (fMRI), positron emission tomography (PET), and electroencephalography (EEG) have revolutionized the field, providing detailed images and measurements of brain activity. These technologies enable researchers to observe how the brain responds to different tasks and stimuli, deepening our understanding of its complex workings. Such advancements have also facilitated the study of neuroplasticity, the brain's ability to reorganize itself by forming new neural connections in response to learning, experience, or injury.

Neuropsychology has wide-ranging applications across multiple domains. In clinical settings, neuropsychologists assess and treat patients with neurological conditions such as traumatic brain injury, stroke, epilepsy, and neurodegenerative diseases like Alzheimer's and Parkinson's. Through cognitive and behavioral assessments, they diagnose impairments, develop rehabilitation strategies, and monitor patients' progress. Their work is crucial in helping individuals regain functionality and improve their quality of life.

In educational environments, neuropsychologists play a pivotal role in identifying and addressing learning disabilities. By understanding the neurocognitive profiles of children with conditions like dyslexia, ADHD, or autism, they develop tailored interventions that support effective learning and development. This work not only aids individual students but also informs educational policies and practices, fostering more inclusive and supportive learning environments.

The field of neuropsychology also intersects with mental health, providing insights into the neural underpinnings of psychiatric disorders such as depression, anxiety, and schizophrenia. Neuropsychological research informs the development of therapeutic approaches and interventions, enhancing treatment efficacy and patient outcomes. Moreover, the principles of neuropsychology extend into emerging fields like artificial intelligence, where understanding human cognition can inform the creation of more intuitive and human-like machines.

In conclusion, neuropsychology is a dynamic and ever-evolving field that bridges the gap between brain science and behavior. Its comprehensive approach to understanding the brain's role in shaping our mental and emotional lives offers invaluable insights into the human condition. As research and technology continue to advance, the contributions of neuropsychology will undoubtedly expand, providing deeper understanding and more effective interventions for the myriad ways our brains influence who we are. This chapter sets the stage for a deeper exploration of these themes, offering a foundation for the intricate journey into the science of behavior, cognition, and emotion.

1.1 Definition and Scope

Neuropsychology is a specialized field within psychology and neuroscience that focuses on the relationship between brain function and behavior. It seeks to understand how different brain structures and neural circuits contribute to cognitive processes, emotional regulation, and overall behavior. This interdisciplinary science integrates principles from biology, neurology, psychology, and cognitive science to explore the complexities of the human brain and its impact on behavior.

At its essence, neuropsychology is concerned with how alterations in brain function affect cognitive abilities and behavior. This includes studying the effects of brain injuries, diseases, and developmental disorders on mental processes such as memory, attention, language, and executive functions. Neuropsychologists use a variety of assessment tools, including standardized tests, clinical interviews, and neuroimaging techniques, to evaluate brain-behavior relationships. By examining patients with neurological impairments, neuropsychologists can identify specific brain regions responsible for particular cognitive functions, providing valuable insights into the brain's organizational structure.

The scope of neuropsychology is broad, encompassing both clinical and research domains. Clinically, neuropsychologists work with individuals across the lifespan, from children with developmental disorders to elderly adults with neurodegenerative diseases. They conduct detailed assessments to diagnose cognitive and behavioral disorders, develop treatment plans, and monitor patient progress. This clinical work is crucial in settings such as hospitals, rehabilitation centers, and private practices, where neuropsychologists collaborate with other healthcare professionals to provide comprehensive care.

In the research domain, neuropsychologists investigate the neural underpinnings of cognitive functions and behaviors. They design experiments to understand how brain activity corresponds to different mental processes, often utilizing advanced neuroimaging technologies like functional magnetic resonance imaging (fMRI) and positron emission tomography (PET). These studies contribute to the fundamental understanding of brain-behavior relationships and inform the development of new diagnostic and therapeutic approaches.

Neuropsychology also extends its influence to educational settings, where it addresses learning disabilities and developmental disorders. By assessing the cognitive strengths and weaknesses of students, neuropsychologists can develop individualized educational plans that cater to each student's unique needs. Their work supports teachers and parents in fostering an environment that promotes effective learning and development. Additionally, neuropsychological insights help shape educational policies and practices, promoting more inclusive and accommodating learning environments.

Moreover, the field of neuropsychology plays a significant role in understanding and treating mental health disorders. Research in neuropsychology has revealed how brain dysfunctions contribute to conditions such as depression, anxiety, schizophrenia, and bipolar disorder. These findings guide the development of targeted treatments and interventions, improving patient outcomes. Neuropsychologists also work in therapeutic settings, providing cognitive rehabilitation and psychotherapy to individuals with mental health disorders.

The scope of neuropsychology is continually expanding with advances in technology and scientific understanding. Emerging fields such as neuroinformatics and computational neuroscience are pushing the boundaries of traditional neuropsychology. These areas utilize computational models and large-scale data analysis to explore brain function and behavior, offering new perspectives and methodologies for studying the brain.

In addition, neuropsychology intersects with fields such as artificial intelligence and human-computer interaction. Understanding human cognition and behavior is essential for designing intelligent systems and interfaces that can interact effectively with people. Neuropsychological principles inform the development of technologies that enhance human performance and well-being.

In conclusion, neuropsychology is a dynamic and multifaceted field that bridges the gap between brain science and behavior. Its comprehensive approach to understanding the brain's role in shaping our cognitive and emotional lives offers invaluable insights into the human condition. As research and technology continue to advance, the contributions of neuropsychology will undoubtedly expand, providing deeper understanding and more effective interventions for the myriad ways our brains influence who we are. This chapter sets the stage for a deeper exploration of these themes, offering a foundation for the intricate journey into the science of behavior, cognition, and emotion.

1.2 Historical Perspectives

The field of neuropsychology, while modern in its technological advancements, has roots that trace back to ancient civilizations. The earliest inklings of the brain's significance in governing behavior can be found in ancient Egyptian and Greek texts. The Edwin Smith Papyrus, dating back to 1700 BCE, is one of the earliest medical documents discussing brain injuries and their impact on behavior. Ancient Greek philosophers like Hippocrates and later Galen advanced the idea that the brain was the center of sensation and intelligence, countering the then-prevailing notion that the heart was the seat of thought and emotion.

The Renaissance period marked a significant shift in the understanding of the brain's role in behavior and cognition. Anatomists like Andreas Vesalius began detailed studies of the brain's anatomy, laying the groundwork for future discoveries. However, it was not until the 19th century that neuropsychology began to take shape as a distinct field. This era witnessed several landmark discoveries that established the connection between specific brain regions and functions.

One of the pivotal figures in early neuropsychology was Paul Broca. In 1861, Broca encountered a patient, known as "Tan" due to his limited speech capabilities, he could understand language but could only utter a single syllable. Upon Tan's death, Broca performed an autopsy and discovered a lesion in the left frontal lobe. This area, now known as Broca's area, is associated with language production. Broca's findings provided strong evidence for the localization of brain functions, suggesting that different brain regions control different aspects of behavior and cognition.

Soon after, Carl Wernicke identified another critical language area in the brain. In 1874, Wernicke studied patients who could speak fluently but made little sense and had difficulty understanding spoken language. He found lesions in the left temporal lobe, an area now known as Wernicke's area, crucial for language comprehension. Together, the discoveries of Broca and Wernicke laid the foundation for understanding the brain's role in language processing and the broader concept of functional localization.

The early 20th century saw further advancements with the work of Russian neuropsychologist Alexander Luria. Luria's studies on brain-injured soldiers during World War II provided significant insights into the brain's functional organization. He developed a theory of brain functioning that emphasized the importance of complex neural networks over isolated brain regions. Luria's approach highlighted the dynamic and interconnected nature of brain functions, paving the way for modern neuropsychological assessments and rehabilitation techniques.

The mid-20th century brought the advent of neuroimaging technologies, revolutionizing the field of neuropsychology. Techniques such as electroencephalography (EEG), which measures electrical activity in the brain, and computed tomography (CT) scans, which provide detailed brain images, allowed scientists to study the brain in unprecedented detail. The introduction of magnetic resonance imaging (MRI) and positron emission tomography (PET) further advanced the ability to observe brain structure and function in real time. These technologies have enabled researchers to correlate specific cognitive functions with distinct brain regions more accurately.

In recent decades, functional MRI (fMRI) has become a cornerstone of neuropsychological research, allowing scientists to observe brain activity associated with various cognitive tasks. This non-invasive technique measures changes in blood flow to different brain regions, providing insights into how the brain processes information and responds to stimuli. Advances in neuroimaging have also facilitated the study of neuroplasticity, demonstrating how the brain can reorganize itself in response to injury, learning, or experience.

The historical progression of neuropsychology from ancient observations to modern technological advancements reflects a deepening understanding of the brain's role in behavior and cognition. The field continues to evolve, driven by ongoing research and technological innovations, promising to unlock further mysteries of the human brain and its intricate connection to our thoughts, emotions, and actions.

1.3 Key Theories and Models

The field of neuropsychology is underpinned by several key theories and models that have shaped our understanding of the brain-behavior relationship. These frameworks provide a foundation for exploring how various brain structures and processes contribute to cognitive functions, emotions, and behaviors.

One of the seminal theories in neuropsychology is the concept of localization of function, which posits that specific cognitive functions are localized to particular areas of the brain. This theory gained prominence in the 19th century with the discoveries of Paul Broca and Carl Wernicke. Broca's identification of a region in the left frontal lobe responsible for speech production and Wernicke's discovery of a region in the left temporal lobe critical for language comprehension provided compelling evidence for this theory. The concept of localization of function has been instrumental in mapping the brain and understanding how different regions contribute to various cognitive and behavioral processes.

Building on the idea of localization, the distributed network model suggests that cognitive functions result from the interaction of multiple brain regions working in concert rather than isolated areas. This model is supported by the work of Russian neuropsychologist Alexander Luria, who emphasized the importance of complex neural networks. Luria's theory proposed that the brain operates as an integrated system, with higher-order cognitive functions arising from the coordinated activity of different brain regions. This perspective has been reinforced by modern neuroimaging techniques, which have revealed the intricate connectivity of the brain's neural networks.

Another influential model is the dual-process theory, which distinguishes between two types of cognitive processing: automatic and controlled. Automatic processes are fast, unconscious, and require minimal cognitive resources, whereas controlled processes are slow, conscious, and resource-intensive. This theory helps explain how we can perform familiar tasks effortlessly while requiring significant effort for novel or complex tasks. The dual-process theory has been applied to various domains, including attention, memory, and decision-making, highlighting the dynamic interplay between different types of cognitive processes.

The cognitive neuropsychological model focuses on understanding cognitive functions through the study of individuals with brain injuries or neurological disorders. By examining patterns of cognitive deficits and preserved abilities, researchers can infer the underlying cognitive architecture and brain organization. This approach has led to the development of detailed cognitive models that describe the components and processes involved in specific functions, such as memory or language. For example, studies of patients with different types of aphasia have provided insights into the modular organization of language processing in the brain.

The neuro constructivist approach emphasizes the role of developmental processes in shaping cognitive functions and brain structures. According to this theory, cognitive abilities and neural architecture emerge from the dynamic interaction between genetic, environmental, and experiential factors during development. Neuroconstructivism highlights the importance of critical periods in development, where the brain is particularly sensitive to specific types of input. This perspective underscores the plasticity of the developing brain and the potential for interventions to enhance cognitive and behavioral outcomes.

The concept of neuroplasticity, the brain's ability to reorganize itself in response to injury, learning, or experience, is another key theory in neuropsychology. Neuroplasticity challenges the notion that the adult brain is fixed and unchangeable, demonstrating that it can adapt and rewire itself throughout life. This theory has profound implications for rehabilitation and therapy, suggesting that targeted interventions can promote recovery and functional improvement in individuals with brain injuries or neurological disorders.

Finally, the biopsychosocial model integrates biological, psychological, and social factors in understanding health and illness. This holistic approach recognizes that cognitive and behavioral functions are influenced by a complex interplay of genetic predispositions, psychological states, and social environments. The biopsychosocial model is widely used in clinical neuropsychology to guide assessment, diagnosis, and treatment, emphasizing the need for comprehensive and individualized care.

These key theories and models collectively enhance our understanding of the brain and its role in shaping cognition and behavior. They provide a framework for exploring the complex interactions between neural structures, cognitive processes, and environmental influences, offering insights into both normal brain function and the impact of neurological disorders.

1.4 Methods and Tools in Neuropsychology

Neuropsychology employs a diverse array of methods and tools to study the relationship between brain function and behavior. These techniques range from clinical assessments and behavioral tests to advanced neuroimaging and electrophysiological methods, each contributing unique insights into brain-behavior dynamics.

Clinical neuropsychological assessment is one of the primary methods used in the field. Neuropsychologists administer standardized tests to evaluate various cognitive domains, including memory, attention, language, executive functions, and visuospatial abilities. These assessments help identify cognitive deficits, guide diagnoses, and inform treatment plans. Tests like the Wechsler Adult Intelligence Scale (WAIS) and the Boston Naming Test are widely used to measure intellectual functioning and language abilities, respectively. Through detailed analysis of test performance, neuropsychologists can infer the integrity of specific brain regions and networks.

Behavioral observation is another fundamental tool in neuropsychology. By systematically observing a patient's behavior during tasks and in naturalistic settings, neuropsychologists gain valuable information about cognitive functioning and adaptive behaviors. This method is particularly useful for assessing individuals who may have difficulty with standardized testing, such as young children or those with severe neurological impairments. Behavioral observations can provide insights into attention, problem-solving strategies, social interactions, and emotional regulation.

Neuroimaging techniques have revolutionized neuropsychology by allowing researchers to visualize and measure brain structure and function in vivo. Structural imaging methods, such as magnetic resonance imaging (MRI) and computed tomography (CT) scans, provide detailed images of brain anatomy, enabling the identification of lesions, atrophy, and other structural abnormalities. Functional imaging techniques, such as functional MRI (fMRI) and positron emission tomography (PET), measure brain activity by detecting changes in blood flow or metabolic processes. These techniques are instrumental in mapping brain functions to specific regions and networks, enhancing our understanding of the neural underpinnings of cognition and behavior.

Electrophysiological methods, including electroencephalography (EEG) and magnetoencephalography (MEG), measure electrical activity in the brain. EEG records the brain's electrical signals via electrodes placed on the scalp, providing high-temporal resolution data on neural activity. It is particularly useful for studying the timing of cognitive processes and identifying abnormalities in brain function, such as epileptic activity. MEG, on the other hand, measures the magnetic fields generated by neural activity, offering better spatial resolution than EEG. These techniques are invaluable for investigating the dynamics of brain activity in real time and understanding the neural mechanisms underlying cognitive functions.

Neuropsychological research also utilizes experimental methods to explore brain-behavior relationships. Controlled experiments involving tasks designed to isolate specific cognitive processes are conducted to understand how different brain regions contribute to these functions. Techniques such as transcranial magnetic stimulation (TMS) and transcranial direct current stimulation (tDCS) are employed to modulate neural activity non-invasively. TMS uses magnetic fields to induce electrical currents in targeted brain areas, temporarily enhancing or inhibiting their activity. tDCS applies a low electrical current to the scalp, altering neuronal excitability. These methods help elucidate causal relationships between brain regions and cognitive functions by observing the effects of stimulation on task performance.

Neuropsychologists also rely on case studies to deepen their understanding of brain-behavior relationships. Detailed examinations of individuals with brain injuries or neurological conditions provide insights into the functions of specific brain areas and the consequences of their impairment. Famous case studies, such as that of Phineas Gage, whose personality changed dramatically after a frontal lobe injury, have significantly contributed to our knowledge of brain function.

In addition to these methods, neuropsychology increasingly incorporates computational modeling and neuroinformatics to analyze complex data and simulate brain functions. Computational models help in understanding how neural circuits process information and generate behavior, while neuroinformatics tools manage and analyze large datasets from neuroimaging and electrophysiological studies.

In conclusion, the methods and tools used in neuropsychology are diverse and complementary, providing a comprehensive understanding of the brain and its role in cognition and behavior. From clinical assessments and behavioral observations to advanced neuroimaging and electrophysiological techniques, each method contributes unique insights that collectively advance the field. These tools enable neuropsychologists to diagnose and treat cognitive disorders, investigate the neural basis of mental processes, and enhance our overall understanding of the human brain.

Chapter 2: Brain Anatomy and Function

The human brain is an intricate and complex organ, central to our thoughts, emotions, and behaviors. Understanding its anatomy and function is crucial for unraveling the mysteries of how we perceive, interact with, and respond to the world around us. This chapter provides an overview of the brain's structure, its major regions, and the functions associated with these areas.

The brain is divided into several regions, each responsible for specific functions. Broadly, it can be categorized into the cerebrum, cerebellum, and brainstem. The cerebrum, the largest part, is divided into two hemispheres, each controlling the opposite side of the body. These hemispheres are further divided into four lobes: frontal, parietal, temporal, and occipital.

The frontal lobe, located at the front of the brain, is crucial for executive functions such as decision-making, problem-solving, planning, and social behavior. It also contains the primary motor cortex, which controls voluntary movements. The prefrontal cortex, part of the frontal lobe, is particularly important for complex cognitive behavior and personality expression. Damage to this area can result in changes in personality, impaired judgment, and difficulty in planning.

The parietal lobe, situated behind the frontal lobe, processes sensory information such as touch, temperature, and pain. It is also involved in spatial orientation and coordination. The somatosensory cortex, located in the parietal lobe, receives and interprets sensory information from various parts of the body. This region helps us understand where our body is in space and how we interact with our environment.

The temporal lobe, located on the sides of the brain, is involved in processing auditory information and is also critical for memory and language comprehension. The hippocampus, found within the temporal lobe, plays a key role in the formation of new memories. The Wernicke's area, also in the temporal lobe, is essential for understanding spoken language. Damage to this area can result in difficulties in language comprehension and production.

The occipital lobe, at the back of the brain, is primarily responsible for visual processing. It contains the primary visual cortex, which receives and interprets information from the eyes. Lesions in this area can lead to visual disturbances or even blindness.

The cerebellum, located underneath the cerebrum, is responsible for coordinating voluntary movements, balance, and posture. It ensures that our movements are smooth and precise. Although smaller than the cerebrum, the cerebellum contains more neurons and plays a crucial role in motor control.

The brainstem, at the base of the brain, connects the brain to the spinal cord. It controls vital life functions such as heart rate, breathing, and blood pressure. The brainstem is divided into three parts: the midbrain, pons, and medulla oblongata. The midbrain is involved in vision, hearing, and motor control. The pons act as a bridge between different parts of the brain, aiding in the control of sleep and respiration. The medulla oblongata regulates autonomic functions, including heartbeat and breathing.

Beneath these larger structures lies the limbic system, often referred to as the "emotional brain." It includes structures such as the amygdala, hippocampus, and hypothalamus, which are essential for emotion regulation, memory, and autonomic functions. The amygdala is crucial for processing emotions like fear and pleasure, while the hypothalamus maintains homeostasis by regulating hunger, thirst, sleep, and hormonal activity.

Neurotransmitters, the brain's chemical messengers, play a vital role in transmitting signals across synapses. Key neurotransmitters include dopamine, which is involved in reward and motivation; serotonin, which regulates mood and sleep; and acetylcholine, which is essential for learning and memory.

Understanding the anatomy and function of the brain provides the foundation for exploring how its different parts work together to produce a vast array of human experiences. This knowledge is critical for diagnosing and treating neurological and psychiatric disorders, guiding research into brain function, and developing new therapeutic interventions. The brain's complexity and its remarkable capabilities continue to be a focal point of scientific inquiry, promising further discoveries that will deepen our understanding of what it means to be human.

2.1 Overview of Brain Structure

The human brain, an organ of extraordinary complexity, serves as the command center for the nervous system. Encased in the skull, it weighs about three pounds and consists of an intricate network of neurons and glial cells that process and transmit information. The brain is divided into several main regions, each with distinct structures and functions, working together to regulate bodily processes and enable cognition, emotion, and behavior.

At the highest level of organization, the brain is divided into three main parts: the cerebrum, cerebellum, and brainstem. The cerebrum, the largest part of the brain, is responsible for higher brain functions such as thought, action, and sensory processing. It is divided into two hemispheres, the left and right, which communicate via the corpus callosum, a thick band of nerve fibers. Each hemisphere is further divided into four lobes: frontal, parietal, temporal, and occipital.

The frontal lobe, located at the front of the brain, is essential for executive functions such as decision-making, problem-solving, and planning. It also contains the primary motor cortex, which controls voluntary movements. The prefrontal cortex, a part of the frontal lobe, is crucial for personality expression and complex cognitive behavior. The parietal lobe, positioned behind the frontal lobe, processes sensory information related to touch, temperature, and pain. It includes the somatosensory cortex, which interprets input from various parts of the body, helping us understand spatial relationships and body positioning.

The temporal lobe, found on the sides of the brain, plays a key role in auditory processing, memory, and language comprehension. It houses the hippocampus, which is vital for forming new memories, and Wernicke's area, critical for language comprehension. The occipital lobe, located at the back of the brain, is primarily involved in visual processing. It contains the primary visual cortex, which interprets information from the eyes, enabling us to perceive and respond to visual stimuli.

Beneath the cerebrum lies the cerebellum, which coordinates voluntary movements, balance, and posture. Despite its smaller size compared to the cerebrum, the cerebellum contains a dense network of neurons and is essential for fine-tuning motor activities and ensuring smooth, coordinated movements.

The brainstem, situated at the base of the brain and connecting to the spinal cord, controls vital life functions such as heart rate, breathing, and blood pressure. It is divided into three parts: the midbrain, pons, and medulla oblongata. The midbrain is involved in motor control, vision, and hearing, while the pons act as a relay station between different parts of the brain, assisting in the control of sleep and respiration. The medulla oblongata regulates autonomic functions, including heartbeat and respiration, and serves as a pathway for nerve signals between the brain and spinal cord.

Deep within the brain lies the limbic system, often referred to as the "emotional brain." This system includes structures such as the amygdala, hippocampus, and hypothalamus. The amygdala is essential for processing emotions such as fear and pleasure, while the hippocampus plays a crucial role in memory formation and spatial navigation. The hypothalamus, a small but vital structure, maintains homeostasis by regulating hunger, thirst, sleep, body temperature, and hormonal activity through its control over the pituitary gland.

Neurotransmitters are the brain's chemical messengers, playing a pivotal role in transmitting signals between neurons. Key neurotransmitters include dopamine, which is involved in reward and motivation; serotonin, which regulates mood, sleep, and appetite; and acetylcholine, which is critical for learning and memory.

In summary, the brain's structure is a highly organized and interrelated system that supports the vast array of human experiences. Each region, from the large lobes of the cerebrum to the intricate circuits of the limbic system, contributes to our ability to think, feel, and interact with the world. Understanding the brain's anatomy is fundamental to exploring its functions and addressing neurological and psychiatric conditions.

2.2 Major Brain Regions and Their Functions

The human brain, a marvel of biological engineering, consists of several major regions, each playing crucial roles in various cognitive and physiological functions. Understanding these regions and their functions is fundamental to comprehending how the brain governs our thoughts, emotions, and behaviors.

The cerebrum is the largest part of the brain and is responsible for most higher-order brain functions. It is divided into two hemispheres—left and right—each controlling the opposite side of the body. These hemispheres are further divided into four lobes: frontal, parietal, temporal, and occipital.

The frontal lobe, located at the front of the brain, is essential for executive functions such as decision-making, problem-solving, planning, and social behavior. It also contains the primary motor cortex, which controls voluntary muscle movements. Within the frontal lobe, the prefrontal cortex is crucial for complex cognitive behavior, personality expression, and moderating social behavior. This area is involved in managing higher-level processes like reasoning, judgment, and impulse control. Damage to the frontal lobe can result in changes to personality, difficulties with planning and organizing, and impaired decision-making.

The parietal lobe, situated behind the frontal lobe, processes sensory information from various parts of the body. It includes the somatosensory cortex, which receives and interprets information related to touch, temperature, pain, and proprioception (the sense of body position). The parietal lobe is also involved in spatial orientation and coordination, allowing us to navigate our environment and understand spatial relationships. Damage to this area can lead to difficulties with spatial awareness, such as not recognizing parts of one's own body or misjudging distances.

The temporal lobe, located on the sides of the brain, plays a key role in processing auditory information and is also crucial for memory and language comprehension. It contains the primary auditory cortex, which is responsible for hearing. The hippocampus, located within the temporal lobe, is vital for forming new memories and spatial navigation. Another important area, Wernicke's area, is involved in understanding spoken language. Damage to the temporal lobe can result in memory problems, difficulties in understanding language (Wernicke's aphasia), and challenges in recognizing sounds and faces.

The occipital lobe, at the back of the brain, is primarily involved in visual processing. It contains the primary visual cortex, which receives and interprets information from the eyes, enabling us to perceive and respond to visual stimuli. Damage to the occipital lobe can lead to visual disturbances or blindness.

Beneath the cerebrum lies the cerebellum, which is crucial for coordinating voluntary movements, balance, and posture. Despite its smaller size, the cerebellum contains a dense network of neurons and plays a vital role in motor control. It ensures that movements are smooth and precise. Damage to the cerebellum can result in uncoordinated movements, difficulty with balance, and impaired motor learning.

The brainstem, located at the base of the brain and connecting to the spinal cord, controls many vital life functions. It is divided into three parts: the midbrain, pons, and medulla oblongata. The midbrain is involved in motor control, vision, and auditory processing. The pons act as a bridge between different parts of the brain and play a role in regulating sleep and respiration. The medulla oblongata controls autonomic functions such as heart rate, breathing, and blood pressure. Damage to the brainstem can be life-threatening, as it controls essential bodily functions.

The limbic system, often referred to as the "emotional brain," includes structures such as the amygdala, hippocampus, and hypothalamus. The amygdala is essential for processing emotions like fear and pleasure, while the hippocampus is crucial for memory formation and spatial navigation. The hypothalamus maintains homeostasis by regulating hunger, thirst, sleep, body temperature, and hormonal activity through its control over the pituitary gland. Dysfunction in the limbic system can lead to emotional disorders, memory problems, and imbalances in bodily functions.

Understanding the major brain regions and their functions is critical for diagnosing and treating neurological and psychiatric conditions. It also provides insight into how the brain orchestrates the complex array of human experiences, from basic physiological processes to higher cognitive functions.

2.3 Neural Communication: Neurons and Synapses

Neural communication forms the foundation of how information is processed and transmitted within the brain and nervous system. This intricate process involves specialized cells called neurons and their connections known as synapses, which enable the transmission of electrical and chemical signals essential for cognition, behavior, and bodily functions.

Neurons are the fundamental units of the nervous system responsible for transmitting information. They come in various shapes and sizes but share common structural features. A typical neuron consists of three main parts: the cell body (soma), dendrites, and an axon. The cell body contains the nucleus and other organelles necessary for cellular functions. Dendrites extend from the cell body and receive incoming signals from other neurons or sensory receptors. These signals are transmitted electrically through the neuron towards the cell body. The axon is a long, slender projection that carries electrical signals away from the cell body to other neurons, muscles, or glands.

Neurons communicate with each other and transmit information through a process known as synaptic transmission. At the junction between neurons, called the synapse, communication occurs through both electrical and chemical signals. Electrical signals travel along the axon of the presynaptic neuron to reach the synaptic terminal, where they trigger the release of neurotransmitters stored in synaptic vesicles. Neurotransmitters are chemical messengers that carry signals across the synaptic gap to the dendrites or cell body of the postsynaptic neuron.

The transmission of signals across the synapse follows a precise sequence of events. When an electrical signal, known as an action potential, reaches the synaptic terminal, it causes voltage-gated calcium channels to open. Calcium ions influx into the terminal, triggering the fusion of synaptic vesicles with the presynaptic membrane. This fusion releases neurotransmitters into the synaptic cleft, the narrow space between the presynaptic and postsynaptic neurons. Neurotransmitters then bind to receptor molecules on the postsynaptic neuron's dendrites or cell body, initiating a response in the postsynaptic neuron.

The binding of neurotransmitters to receptors can lead to excitatory or inhibitory effects on the postsynaptic neuron. Excitatory neurotransmitters, such as glutamate, increase the likelihood that the postsynaptic neuron will generate an action potential, thereby enhancing neural communication. In contrast, inhibitory neurotransmitters, such as gamma-aminobutyric acid (GABA), decrease the likelihood of an action potential, regulating neural activity and preventing overexcitation.

After neurotransmitter binding, several mechanisms can terminate synaptic transmission and regulate neural activity. Reuptake is one such mechanism, where neurotransmitters are reabsorbed by the presynaptic neuron's terminal through transporter proteins. Enzymatic degradation breaks down neurotransmitters into inactive metabolites, which are then recycled or eliminated. Diffusion allows neurotransmitters to drift away from the synapse, reducing their concentration and terminating their effects on the postsynaptic neuron.

Neurons are organized into complex networks that facilitate information processing and communication throughout the brain and nervous system. These networks form the basis for cognitive functions such as perception, memory, learning, and decision-making. The brain's ability to adapt and change in response to experiences, known as neuroplasticity, relies on the dynamic nature of synaptic connections. Synaptic plasticity refers to the ability of synapses to strengthen or weaken over time in response to activity, contributing to learning and memory formation.

Disruptions in neural communication can lead to neurological disorders and cognitive deficits. For example, abnormalities in neurotransmitter systems are implicated in conditions such as Alzheimer's disease, Parkinson's disease, and schizophrenia. Understanding the mechanisms of neural communication, including the role of neurons and synapses, is essential for advancing treatments and interventions for these disorders.

In conclusion, neurons and synapses are integral components of neural communication, enabling the brain to process information and coordinate complex behaviors. Their precise interactions and regulation ensure the efficient transmission of signals critical for maintaining bodily functions and supporting cognitive processes essential for the human experience.

2.4 Neuroplasticity: The Brain's Ability to Change

Neuroplasticity refers to the brain's remarkable ability to reorganize itself in response to internal and external stimuli, forming new neural connections and adapting its structure and function throughout life. This concept challenges the traditional view that the brain's structure and function are fixed in adulthood, highlighting instead its dynamic nature and capacity for both adaptive and maladaptive changes.

Types of Neuroplasticity

1. **Structural Plasticity**: This form of neuroplasticity involves physical changes in the brain's structure, including the formation of

new dendrites and synapses, as well as alterations in axonal branching. Structural plasticity enables the brain to reorganize its neural networks in response to learning, experience, and environmental factors. For example, studies have shown that practicing a new skill, such as playing a musical instrument or learning a new language, can lead to structural changes in relevant brain regions, enhancing functional abilities associated with those skills.

2. **Functional Plasticity**: Functional plasticity refers to the brain's ability to redistribute tasks across different areas in response to damage or sensory deprivation. When a particular brain region is compromised due to injury or disease, neighboring regions may assume its functions to compensate for the loss. This phenomenon is often observed in individuals recovering from stroke or traumatic brain injury, where intact brain areas reorganize to restore lost functions, such as movement or language abilities.

3. **Synaptic Plasticity**: Synaptic plasticity involves changes in the strength and efficacy of synaptic connections between neurons. It underlies learning and memory processes by facilitating the modification of existing synapses or the formation of new synaptic connections. Long-term potentiation (LTP) and long-term depression (LTD) are mechanisms of synaptic plasticity that enhance or weaken synaptic transmission, respectively, in response to patterns of neuronal activity. These processes are crucial for encoding experiences into memory and refining neural circuits involved in cognitive functions.

Mechanisms of Neuroplasticity

1. **Hebbian Plasticity**: Coined by psychologist Donald Hebb, the principle of "cells that fire together wire together" encapsulates the

concept of Hebbian plasticity. This mechanism suggests that synaptic connections strengthen when neurons repeatedly fire in close temporal proximity, reinforcing the association between neurons and facilitating learning and memory formation.

2. **Neurotransmitter Regulation**: Neuroplasticity is influenced by the activity of neurotransmitters, chemical messengers that transmit signals between neurons. For example, dopamine plays a critical role in reward-based learning and motivation, influencing synaptic plasticity in brain regions associated with these functions. Serotonin regulates mood and emotional processing, impacting synaptic plasticity in circuits involved in emotional regulation and stress response.

3. **Environmental Enrichment**: Environmental factors such as sensory stimulation, social interactions, and cognitive engagement can promote neuroplasticity by enhancing synaptic connectivity and promoting the survival of neurons. Studies in animal models have demonstrated that exposure to enriched environments, characterized by complex stimuli and opportunities for physical activity and social interaction, leads to structural and functional changes in the brain that support cognitive resilience and adaptive behaviors.

Applications and Implications

Understanding neuroplasticity has profound implications for education, rehabilitation, and the treatment of neurological and psychiatric disorders. Educational strategies that capitalize on neuroplasticity, such as interactive learning environments and personalized instruction, can optimize learning outcomes by fostering synaptic connections and neural circuits associated with academic skills.

In clinical settings, therapies aimed at promoting neuroplasticity are integral to rehabilitation programs for individuals recovering from stroke, traumatic brain injury, or neurodevelopmental disorders. Techniques such as constraint-induced movement therapy and cognitive rehabilitation harness neuroplastic mechanisms to enhance motor function and cognitive abilities, respectively.

Furthermore, research into neuroplasticity holds promise for developing interventions to mitigate the effects of neurodegenerative diseases and mental health disorders. Strategies targeting synaptic plasticity and neurogenesis, the generation of new neurons, are being explored as potential treatments for conditions such as Alzheimer's disease, depression, and anxiety disorders.

In conclusion, neuroplasticity underscores the brain's capacity for adaptation and renewal throughout life, shaping our ability to learn, recover from injury, and adapt to changing environments. By unraveling the mechanisms of neuroplasticity, researchers and clinicians are paving the way for innovative approaches to enhance brain function, resilience, and well-being across the lifespan.

Chapter 3: Cognitive Processes and Brain Function

Cognitive processes encompass a broad range of mental activities that enable us to perceive, understand, remember, and respond to information from our environment. These processes are intricately linked to brain function, involving specialized neural circuits and regions that work together to support various cognitive functions. Understanding the relationship between cognitive processes and brain function sheds light on how the brain orchestrates complex behaviors and mental activities.

Perception is the initial stage of cognitive processing, where sensory information from the environment is detected and interpreted by the brain. Visual perception, for example, involves the activation of the occipital lobe, specifically the primary visual cortex, which receives and processes visual input from the eyes. The temporal lobe contributes to auditory perception, while the parietal lobe integrates sensory information to create a cohesive understanding of the environment.

Attention directs cognitive resources towards specific stimuli or tasks, enabling focused processing and filtering out irrelevant information. The frontal and parietal lobes play crucial roles in attentional control, regulating the allocation of attention and maintaining cognitive vigilance. Neuroimaging studies have shown that the prefrontal cortex, in particular, coordinates attention networks across the brain, allowing individuals to prioritize information and tasks based on goals and relevance.

Memory involves the encoding, storage, and retrieval of information, essential for learning and adaptive behavior. The hippocampus, located within the temporal lobe, is critical for forming new memories and spatial navigation. Memory processes rely on synaptic plasticity and neural circuits that link different brain regions involved in encoding sensory information, consolidating memories during sleep, and retrieving stored information during recall.

Language is a complex cognitive function that involves the comprehension and production of spoken and written communication. Wernicke's area, located in the left temporal lobe, is crucial for understanding language, while Broca's area, in the left frontal lobe, coordinates speech production. The integration of language processes spans multiple brain regions, including the parietal and occipital lobes, enabling the processing of linguistic information and communication.

Executive functions encompass higher-order cognitive processes that facilitate goal-directed behavior, decision-making, and problem-solving. The prefrontal cortex, extensively interconnected with other brain regions, plays a central role in executive function by integrating sensory information, regulating emotional responses, and planning complex tasks. Dysfunction in executive function can manifest in difficulties with impulse control, organization, and cognitive flexibility.

Emotion regulation involves the cognitive and neural processes that govern emotional responses and adaptive behavior in social and environmental contexts. The amygdala, part of the limbic system, plays a crucial role in processing emotions such as fear and pleasure, while the prefrontal cortex modulates emotional responses and regulates behavior based on social norms and personal goals.

Decision-making is a cognitive process that integrates sensory information, past experiences, and emotional responses to select optimal actions or choices. Decision-making involves interactions between the prefrontal cortex, which evaluates options and predicts outcomes, and subcortical regions such as the basal ganglia, which facilitate motor responses and reinforcement learning.

Problem-solving encompasses cognitive strategies and mental processes used to overcome obstacles and achieve goals. The frontal and parietal lobes contribute to problem-solving by enabling analytical reasoning, spatial cognition, and working memory. Problem-solving tasks activate neural networks involved in planning, hypothesis testing, and evaluating potential solutions.

In summary, cognitive processes are fundamental to human cognition and behavior, underpinned by complex interactions between neural circuits and brain regions specialized for perception, attention, memory, language, executive functions, emotion regulation, decision-making, and problem-solving. The study of cognitive processes and brain function continues to advance our understanding of the neural basis of cognition, inform educational practices, and guide interventions for neurological and psychiatric disorders. Integrating research from cognitive neuroscience, psychology, and neurobiology provides a comprehensive framework for exploring how the brain supports diverse cognitive functions and adapts to changes in the environment across the lifespan.

3.1 Attention and Perception

Attention and perception are essential cognitive processes that work in tandem to facilitate our interaction with the environment, guiding what information we perceive and how we interpret it. These processes are intricately linked to brain function, involving specialized neural mechanisms and networks that enable us to selectively attend to relevant stimuli and integrate sensory information into coherent perceptions.

Attention is the cognitive ability to focus mental resources on specific stimuli or tasks while ignoring irrelevant or distracting information. It plays a crucial role in enhancing perception, memory, and decision-making by prioritizing sensory input and regulating cognitive resources. Attention can be broadly categorized into several types, including selective attention, sustained attention, divided attention, and executive attention.

Selective attention allows individuals to concentrate on specific stimuli while filtering out competing distractions. This process is essential for maintaining focus in noisy or complex environments, such as listening to a conversation in a crowded room. Neuroimaging studies have identified brain regions involved in selective attention, including the frontal and parietal lobes, which regulate attentional control and prioritize sensory processing based on task demands and goals.

Sustained attention, also known as vigilance, refers to the ability to maintain focus and concentration over extended periods. It is crucial for tasks that require prolonged mental effort, such as reading a book or monitoring for changes in a visual display. The frontal cortex, particularly the dorsolateral prefrontal cortex, plays a significant role in sustaining attention by monitoring task-relevant information and adjusting cognitive resources to maintain optimal performance.

Divided attention involves multitasking or simultaneously attending to multiple stimuli or tasks. It requires the coordination of attentional resources and the ability to allocate mental effort efficiently across different activities. The parietal lobe and superior colliculus are implicated in divided attention, facilitating the rapid shifting of attention between stimuli and coordinating sensory processing across sensory modalities.

Executive attention encompasses higher-order processes that enable flexible and goal-directed behavior. It involves inhibitory control, cognitive flexibility, and the ability to suppress irrelevant information while focusing on task-relevant goals. The anterior cingulate cortex and lateral prefrontal cortex are critical for executive attention, regulating attentional shifts, and resolving conflicts between competing stimuli or responses.

Perception, on the other hand, involves the process of interpreting sensory information to form mental representations of the external world. It encompasses various sensory modalities, including vision, hearing, and touch, taste, and smell, each involving specialized sensory systems and brain regions.

Visual perception relies on the complex processing of visual information by the occipital lobe and associated visual cortex. The primary visual cortex, located in the occipital lobe, receives input from the eyes and analyzes visual features such as shape, color, and motion. Higher-order visual areas, such as the ventral and dorsal streams, integrate this information to recognize objects, navigate spatial environments, and guide visually guided actions.

Auditory perception involves the processing of sound waves by the auditory system, located in the temporal lobe. The primary auditory cortex analyzes auditory input, including pitch, intensity, and spatial location. Auditory information is further processed in higher-order auditory areas, facilitating speech perception, sound localization, and auditory scene analysis.

Somatosensory perception encompasses the processing of tactile sensations, proprioception (body position), and nociception (pain) by sensory receptors in the skin, muscles, and joints. The parietal lobe, including the somatosensory cortex, interprets somatosensory input and integrates sensory information to perceive touch, temperature, pressure, and body position.

Perceptual processes are influenced by top-down and bottom-up mechanisms. Top-down processing involves the influence of prior knowledge, expectations, and cognitive factors on perceptual interpretation. For example, contextual cues and past experiences can shape how we perceive ambiguous stimuli or interpret sensory information in familiar contexts.

Bottom-up processing, in contrast, involves the direct processing of sensory input from external stimuli. It begins with sensory receptors detecting physical stimuli and transmitting neural signals to higher-order brain regions for analysis and interpretation. Bottom-up processing is essential for detecting novel stimuli and responding to changes in the environment.

In conclusion, attention and perception are fundamental cognitive processes that enable us to interact effectively with our surroundings, guiding our behavior, decisions, and understanding of the world. These processes rely on specialized neural mechanisms and interactions between brain regions involved in sensory processing, attentional control, and cognitive regulation. Understanding the neural basis of attention and perception provides insights into how the brain filters and interprets sensory information, paving the way for advancements in education, rehabilitation, and interventions for neurological and psychiatric disorders.

3.2 Memory Systems: Short-term and Long-term Memory

Memory is a fundamental cognitive function that allows us to encode, store, and retrieve information over time. The process of memory involves complex interactions between neural circuits and brain regions specialized for different types of memory, including short-term memory (STM) and long-term memory (LTM). Understanding these memory systems provides insights into how the brain organizes and retains information for various cognitive functions.

Short-term Memory (STM), also known as working memory, refers to the temporary storage and manipulation of information needed for ongoing cognitive tasks. STM allows individuals to hold and process information over short intervals, typically ranging from a few seconds to minutes. This capacity is essential for tasks such as mental arithmetic, following directions, and comprehending spoken language in real time.

The prefrontal cortex and parietal cortex play crucial roles in STM by supporting attentional control, cognitive processing, and the maintenance of information in an active state. The prefrontal cortex, particularly the dorsolateral prefrontal cortex, is involved in the rehearsal and manipulation of information held in STM. Neuroimaging studies have shown increased activity in these regions during tasks requiring STM, indicating their involvement in maintaining and updating information over brief periods.

STM operates through a limited capacity and is susceptible to interference and decay without rehearsal or consolidation into long-term memory. Research suggests that STM can hold approximately 7 ± 2 items of information at a time, a concept proposed by psychologist George Miller as the "magic number seven". This capacity can vary depending on factors such as complexity, familiarity, and individual differences in cognitive abilities.

Long-term Memory (LTM) involves the storage of information over extended periods, ranging from hours to a lifetime. LTM encompasses explicit (declarative) and implicit (non-declarative) memory systems, each serving distinct functions and relying on different neural substrates.

Explicit memory refers to the conscious recollection of facts, events, and personal experiences that can be intentionally recalled and articulated. It includes episodic memory, which stores personal experiences and events tied to specific times and places, and semantic memory, which holds general knowledge and factual information about the world. The hippocampus, located in the temporal lobe, plays a critical role in the formation and consolidation of explicit memories, integrating information from various brain regions during encoding and retrieval.

Implicit memory involves unconscious forms of memory that influence behavior, skills, and habits without conscious awareness. Implicit memory includes procedural memory, which enables the performance of learned motor skills and tasks, and emotional memory, which stores associations between stimuli and emotional responses. Implicit memory systems rely on brain regions such as the basal ganglia, cerebellum, and amygdala, which are involved in motor learning, procedural skills, and emotional processing.

The consolidation of memories from STM to LTM involves processes that stabilize and strengthen neural connections over time. Memory consolidation is facilitated by synaptic plasticity, particularly long-term potentiation (LTP), which enhances synaptic efficacy and supports the storage of memories in cortical and subcortical regions.

Encoding, the initial process of forming memories, involves transforming sensory input into a form that can be stored and retrieved. Effective encoding strategies, such as elaboration (connecting new information to existing knowledge), organization (structuring information into meaningful patterns), and visualization (creating mental images), enhance memory retention and retrieval.

Retrieval refers to the process of accessing stored information from memory. Retrieval cues, context, and emotional state influence the accessibility of memories stored in LTM. Retrieval can be enhanced through techniques such as mnemonic devices, retrieval practice (repeated testing), and spaced repetition (reviewing information over spaced intervals).

In summary, memory systems play essential roles in cognitive functioning by enabling the storage, retention, and retrieval of information necessary for learning, decision-making, and adaptive behavior. STM supports temporary cognitive processes, whereas LTM facilitates the long-term storage of factual knowledge, personal experiences, and learned skills. The neural basis of memory involves interactions between cortical and subcortical brain regions specialized for different memory systems, highlighting the dynamic and adaptive nature of human memory processes across the lifespan.

3.3 Language and Communication

Language and communication are foundational aspects of human cognition and social interaction, facilitated by specialized neural circuits and brain regions that support the comprehension, production, and interpretation of spoken and written language. Understanding the neural basis of language provides insights into how the brain processes linguistic information, coordinates speech production, and facilitates meaningful communication.

Neural Basis of Language

Broca's Area, located in the left frontal lobe of the brain, plays a critical role in language production and speech articulation. Named after French neurologist Paul Broca, this region is responsible for coordinating the motor aspects of speech production, including the precise movements of the lips, tongue, and vocal cords needed to produce coherent speech. Damage to Broca's area can result in expressive aphasia, a condition characterized by difficulty in producing fluent speech while maintaining grammatical structure and articulation.

Wernicke 's area, situated in the left temporal lobe adjacent to the auditory cortex, is crucial for language comprehension and understanding. Discovered by German neurologist Carl Wernicke, this region interprets and assigns meaning to auditory information, allowing individuals to comprehend spoken language and process semantic relationships between words. Damage to Wernicke's area can lead to receptive aphasia, impairing the ability to understand spoken and written language despite intact speech production.

Arcuate Fasciculus is a neural pathway that connects Broca's area and Wernicke's area, facilitating the transmission of language-related information between regions responsible for speech production and comprehension. This pathway plays a crucial role in integrating auditory and motor processes during language processing, supporting fluent communication and the coordination of language functions across different brain areas.

Language Processing and Cognitive Functions

Language processing involves a series of interconnected cognitive functions that enable individuals to generate, comprehend, and use language effectively in various contexts:

Phonology refers to the system of sounds that make up language and the rules governing their combination to form words and sentences. The superior temporal gyrus and Heschl's gyrus in the auditory cortex are involved in processing phonological information, allowing individuals to distinguish between different speeches sounds and recognize phonetic patterns.

Syntax involves the rules governing the structure of sentences and the arrangement of words to convey meaning. The left hemisphere, particularly areas adjacent to Broca's area, is specialized for syntactic processing, enabling individuals to parse sentences, understand grammatical relationships, and generate grammatically correct speech.

Semantics encompasses the meaning of words, phrases, and sentences within the context of communication. Semantic processing relies on distributed neural networks that integrate information from Wernicke's area, temporal lobe regions, and the inferior frontal gyrus, supporting the comprehension and interpretation of linguistic meaning.

Pragmatics refers to the social and contextual aspects of language use, including the interpretation of implied meaning, nonverbal cues, and conversational turn-taking. The right hemisphere, in conjunction with frontal and temporal regions, contributes to pragmatic language processing by integrating social information, monitoring conversational norms, and adjusting communication strategies based on situational context.

Language Development and Plasticity

Language acquisition and development involve the interaction between genetic predispositions and environmental influences, shaping neural circuits specialized for language processing from infancy through adulthood. Early language exposure and experience contribute to the refinement and organization of neural networks supporting language functions, promoting linguistic fluency and communicative competence.

Neuroplasticity plays a crucial role in language learning and adaptation, allowing the brain to reorganize and modify neural circuits in response to linguistic experience, bilingualism, and recovery from language impairments. Language rehabilitation strategies, such as speech therapy and language training, leverage neuroplastic mechanisms to promote recovery and enhance communication skills in individuals with aphasia or other language disorders.

In conclusion, language and communication are complex cognitive functions supported by specialized neural systems and brain regions that enable individuals to understand, produce, and interact using spoken and written language. The neural basis of language involves dynamic interactions between cortical and subcortical regions specialized for phonological, syntactic, semantic, and pragmatic aspects of language processing. Understanding the neural mechanisms underlying language provides insights into the cognitive processes essential for human communication, informing educational practices, clinical interventions, and research aimed at unraveling the complexities of language and its impact on cognition and social interaction.

3.4 Executive Functions: Planning, Decision-Making, and Problem-Solving

Executive functions encompass a set of cognitive processes that enable individuals to regulate behavior, plan and execute tasks, make decisions, and solve problems effectively. These higher-order cognitive abilities are crucial for goal-directed behavior, adaptive functioning, and the management of complex tasks in daily life. Executive functions rely on specialized neural circuits and brain regions that coordinate cognitive processes, monitor performance, and facilitate flexible, goal-oriented behavior.

Neural Basis of Executive Functions

The prefrontal Cortex, particularly the dorsolateral prefrontal cortex (DLPFC) and ventromedial prefrontal cortex (VMPFC), plays a central role in executive function by integrating sensory information, coordinating cognitive processes, and regulating behavior based on internal goals and external demands. The DLPFC is involved in planning, working memory, cognitive flexibility, and inhibitory control, supporting the organization and execution of complex tasks. The VMPFC contributes to emotional regulation, social behavior, and decision-making by integrating emotional and motivational factors into executive processes.

Anterior Cingulate Cortex (ACC) is implicated in monitoring and detecting conflicts between competing goals or responses, facilitating error detection, and adjusting behavior accordingly. The ACC plays a crucial role in response inhibition, attentional control, and the evaluation of task performance, contributing to adaptive decision-making and the resolution of cognitive conflicts.

Basal Ganglia and Frontal Striatum are subcortical structures involved in motor control, reward processing, and reinforcement learning, supporting the initiation and execution of goal-directed behaviors. The basal ganglia contribute to procedural memory, habit formation, and the regulation of motor sequences, while the frontal striatum integrates feedback and reward signals to guide decision-making and reinforcement learning processes.

Functions of Executive Processes

Planning involves the formulation of goals, strategies, and action sequences to achieve desired outcomes. Effective planning relies on cognitive processes such as working memory, cognitive flexibility, and foresight, enabling individuals to anticipate future events, allocate resources, and coordinate complex actions. The prefrontal cortex, particularly the DLPFC, coordinates planning by integrating sensory information, evaluating alternatives, and sequencing actions to achieve long-term objectives.

Decision-making encompasses the process of evaluating options, predicting outcomes, and selecting optimal choices based on preferences, values, and goals. Decision-making involves integrating information from sensory input, memory, and emotional responses to weigh potential risks and rewards. The ventromedial prefrontal cortex and orbitofrontal cortex play critical roles in decision-making by encoding value representations, integrating emotional signals, and guiding adaptive choices in uncertain or ambiguous situations.

Problem-solving involves identifying obstacles, generating alternative solutions, and implementing strategies to achieve desired outcomes. Effective problem-solving relies on cognitive flexibility, analytical reasoning, and the ability to overcome cognitive biases and functional fixedness. The prefrontal cortex and anterior cingulate cortex support problem-solving by facilitating cognitive control, monitoring task progress, and adapting strategies based on feedback and environmental demands.

Development and Impairments

Executive functions undergo significant development throughout childhood and adolescence, maturing alongside the prefrontal cortex and neural circuits supporting cognitive control and decision-making. Early experiences, environmental factors, and genetic influences contribute to individual differences in executive functioning, influencing academic achievement, social competence, and adaptive behavior across the lifespan.

Impairments in executive functions are associated with neurodevelopmental disorders such as attention-deficit/hyperactivity disorder (ADHD), autism spectrum disorder (ASD), and specific learning disabilities. These conditions are characterized by difficulties with attentional control, impulse regulation, planning, and problem-solving, impacting academic performance, social interactions, and daily functioning.

Clinical Implications and Interventions

Understanding the neural basis of executive functions informs clinical assessments and interventions aimed at supporting individuals with executive function deficits. Cognitive remediation therapies, behavioral interventions, and pharmacological treatments target specific aspects of executive functioning to improve attentional control, impulse regulation, planning, and decision-making skills in clinical populations.

In conclusion, executive functions are essential cognitive processes supported by specialized neural circuits and brain regions that enable individuals to regulate behavior, plan and execute tasks, make decisions, and solve problems effectively. The prefrontal cortex, anterior cingulate cortex, and basal ganglia play critical roles in coordinating executive processes, monitoring performance, and facilitating adaptive behavior across various domains of cognition and behavior. Enhancing our understanding of executive functions provides insights into cognitive development, clinical disorders, and interventions aimed at optimizing cognitive functioning and adaptive behavior in diverse populations.

Chapter 4: Emotional Processes and Brain Function

Emotional processes are integral to human experience, influencing behavior, decision-making, social interactions, and overall well-being. These processes are supported by a complex interplay of neural circuits and brain regions that regulate emotional responses, interpret social cues, and modulate affective states. Understanding the neural basis of emotional processing provides insights into how the brain orchestrates emotional experiences, shapes behavior, and responds to environmental stimuli.

Neural Basis of Emotional Processing

The amygdala, located within the temporal lobe, plays a central role in emotional processing by detecting and responding to salient stimuli, particularly those associated with threat, reward, or emotional significance. The amygdala receives sensory input from multiple sensory modalities, including visual, auditory, and somatosensory systems, and integrates this information to generate emotional responses and initiate physiological reactions, such as changes in heart rate and hormonal release.

The prefrontal Cortex, including the ventromedial prefrontal cortex (VMPFC) and orbitofrontal cortex (OFC), modulates emotional responses, regulates decision-making, and integrates emotional information with cognitive processes. The VMPFC evaluates the emotional significance of stimuli, encodes reward values, and guides adaptive behavior based on social and emotional context. The OFC integrates sensory information, evaluates the consequences of actions, and facilitates emotional regulation by inhibiting impulsive responses and promoting goal-directed behavior.

Anterior Cingulate Cortex (ACC) is involved in monitoring emotional conflicts, regulating emotional responses, and integrating cognitive and emotional information during decision-making. The ACC plays a critical role in detecting errors, resolving conflicts between competing goals or responses, and modulating emotional arousal to optimize behavioral outcomes in challenging or uncertain situations.

Functions of Emotional Processes

Emotion Regulation encompasses strategies and processes that modulate emotional experiences, responses, and expressions to achieve desired outcomes. Effective emotion regulation involves cognitive processes such as reappraisal (reinterpretation of emotional stimuli), suppression (inhibition of emotional expressions), and distraction (shifting attention away from emotional triggers). The prefrontal cortex, particularly the VMPFC and ACC, plays a key role in implementing emotion regulation strategies, monitoring emotional states, and adjusting behavior based on situational demands.

Social and Interpersonal Behavior involves the interpretation of social cues, emotional expressions, and nonverbal communication signals to navigate social interactions and establish interpersonal relationships. The temporal parietal junction (TPJ) and mirror neuron system are implicated in social cognition by facilitating empathy, perspective-taking, and understanding others' emotional states. These regions support social decision-making, cooperation, and the formation of social bonds essential for adaptive social behavior.

Stress Response and Coping Mechanisms involve physiological and behavioral adaptations to environmental stressors, threats, or challenges. The hypothalamic-pituitary-adrenal (HPA) axis and sympathetic nervous system regulate stress hormone release (e.g., cortisol) and physiological responses (e.g., increased heart rate), mobilizing resources to cope with perceived threats or stressors. Chronic stress can dysregulate these systems, contributing to physical and mental health problems such as anxiety disorders, depression, and cardiovascular disease.

Development and Plasticity

Emotional processes undergo significant development throughout childhood and adolescence, influenced by genetic predispositions, early experiences, and social interactions. The maturation of prefrontal cortex regions involved in emotional regulation, coupled with changes in neural connectivity and synaptic plasticity, supports the refinement of emotional responses, coping strategies, and social-emotional competence across development.

Neuroplasticity enables the brain to adapt and reorganize in response to emotional experiences, learning, and environmental influences. Adaptive changes in neural circuits supporting emotional processing and regulation contribute to resilience, emotional flexibility, and the ability to cope with stress and adversity throughout the lifespan.

Clinical Implications and Interventions

Understanding the neural basis of emotional processes informs clinical assessments and interventions aimed at addressing emotional dysregulation, mood disorders, and trauma-related symptoms. Evidence-based therapies, such as cognitive-behavioral therapy (CBT), dialectical behavior therapy (DBT), and mindfulness-based interventions, target emotion regulation skills, enhance emotional awareness, and promote adaptive coping strategies in clinical populations.

In summary, emotional processes are fundamental to human cognition, behavior, and social interactions, supported by specialized neural circuits and brain regions that regulate emotional responses, interpret social cues, and modulate affective states. The amygdala, prefrontal cortex, anterior cingulate cortex, and other brain regions collaborate to integrate emotional and cognitive processes, facilitating adaptive behavior, emotional regulation, and social functioning across diverse contexts. Enhancing our understanding of emotional processing provides insights into emotional development, mental health disorders, and therapeutic approaches aimed at promoting emotional well-being and resilience in individuals and communities.

4.1 Understanding Emotions: Theories and Models

Understanding emotions involves exploring various theories and models that elucidate the cognitive, physiological, and social aspects of emotional experiences. These frameworks provide insights into how emotions are generated, regulated, and expressed, shedding light on their adaptive functions and implications for human behavior and well-being.

Theories and Models of Emotions

James-Lange Theory

The James-Lange theory of emotions, proposed by William James and Carl Lange in the late 19th century, posits that emotions arise from physiological responses to stimuli in the environment. According to this theory, the sequence of events begins with a physiological reaction (e.g., increased heart rate, sweating), which is then interpreted by the brain as an emotional experience (e.g., fear or excitement). For instance, encountering a bear triggers physiological changes associated with fear, which subsequently leads to the experience of fear itself.

Cannon-Bard Theory

The Cannon-Bard theory, developed by Walter Cannon and later refined by Philip Bard, challenges the James-Lange theory by proposing that emotional responses occur simultaneously with physiological reactions, rather than one causing the other. According to this theory, emotional experiences and physiological responses (e.g., heart rate increase, and sweating) originate from separate but parallel processes within the brain. For example, encountering a threatening situation triggers both the subjective experience of fear and the physiological changes associated with the fight-or-flight response simultaneously.

Schachter-Singer Two-Factor Theory

The Schachter-Singer two-factor theory, also known as the cognitive arousal theory, integrates elements of both the James-Lange and Cannon-Bard theories. Developed by Stanley Schachter and Jerome Singer in the 1960s, this model suggests that emotions result from the interaction between physiological arousal and cognitive interpretation of situational cues. According to this theory, the experience of an emotion depends on two factors: physiological arousal (e.g., increased heart rate) and cognitive appraisal (e.g., interpreting the cause of arousal based on environmental context). For instance, feeling excited or anxious in response to a challenging situation may depend on how one interprets and labels their physiological state.

Appraisal Theories

Appraisal theories of emotions emphasize the role of cognitive appraisal processes in shaping emotional experiences. According to these theories, emotions are elicited by the subjective evaluation or appraisal of the significance of events, situations, or stimuli about one's goals, values, and beliefs. Richard Lazarus proposed that emotions arise from ongoing evaluations of the personal relevance and implications of environmental stimuli. For example, encountering a snake may elicit fear if it is perceived as threatening, but curiosity if it is perceived as non-threatening or interesting.

Evolutionary Theories

Evolutionary theories of emotions propose that emotions have evolved to serve adaptive functions that promote survival and reproductive success. Charles Darwin suggested that emotions, such as fear, anger, and joy, have evolved as adaptive responses to environmental challenges and opportunities. These emotions facilitate responses that enhance survival, social bonding, and reproductive fitness. For example, fear prompts avoidance of dangerous situations, while joy reinforces behaviors that lead to positive outcomes, such as social interaction or mating opportunities.

Cultural and Social Constructivist Perspectives

Cultural and social constructivist perspectives highlight the role of cultural norms, social contexts, and interpersonal relationships in shaping emotional experiences and expressions. These perspectives emphasize that emotions are influenced by cultural values, social norms, and collective beliefs about emotional expression and regulation. Cultural variations in emotional expression, such as display rules governing when and how emotions are expressed, illustrate the impact of social and cultural contexts on emotional experiences.

Understanding emotions through diverse theoretical frameworks enhances our knowledge of how emotions are generated, regulated, and expressed across different contexts and individuals. These theories and models provide complementary perspectives on the cognitive, physiological, evolutionary, and cultural dimensions of emotional experiences, offering insights into the adaptive functions of emotions, their role in social interactions, and implications for psychological well-being. By integrating insights from these theories, researchers and practitioners can deepen their understanding of emotional processes and develop effective interventions for promoting emotional regulation, resilience, and mental health in diverse populations.

4.2 The Role of the Limbic System

The limbic system is a complex network of brain structures involved in a range of functions, including emotions, behavior, motivation, memory, and olfaction (sense of smell). It plays a crucial role in integrating sensory information, regulating emotional responses, and modulating cognitive processes essential for adaptive behavior and survival.

Anatomy of the Limbic System

The limbic system comprises several interconnected structures located within the cerebral hemispheres and subcortical regions of the brain. Key components of the limbic system include:

1. **Hippocampus**: Located within the temporal lobe, the hippocampus is critical for the formation and consolidation of long-term memories, particularly episodic memories related to personal experiences and spatial navigation. The hippocampus also plays a role in spatial learning, cognitive mapping, and contextual memory retrieval.
2. **Amygdala**: Situated within the temporal lobe adjacent to the hippocampus, the amygdala is involved in the processing and regulation of emotions, particularly fear and emotional responses to threatening stimuli. The amygdala receives sensory input from multiple sensory modalities and plays a central role in detecting and responding to salient stimuli, initiating the fight-or-flight response, and modulating emotional arousal.
3. **Hypothalamus**: Located below the thalamus, the hypothalamus serves as a key regulatory center for homeostatic functions, including temperature regulation, hunger and thirst, sleep-wake cycles, and hormone secretion. The hypothalamus also plays a role in emotional responses, particularly in coordinating physiological responses to emotional stimuli through connections with the autonomic nervous system and pituitary gland.
4. **Thalamus**: The thalamus serves as a relay station for sensory information traveling between the cerebral cortex and subcortical structures, including the limbic system. It regulates sensory perception, attention, and awareness by filtering and directing sensory input to relevant cortical areas for further processing.

5. **Cingulate Cortex**: The cingulate cortex, part of the cerebral cortex above the corpus callosum, is involved in emotional regulation, decision-making, and processing of pain and reward signals. The anterior cingulate cortex (ACC) plays a role in monitoring cognitive conflicts, regulating emotional responses, and integrating emotional and cognitive information during decision-making processes.

Functions of the Limbic System

- **Emotional Processing**: The limbic system plays a central role in emotional processing by integrating sensory information with emotional responses and regulating emotional arousal. The amygdala, in particular, processes emotional stimuli and initiates physiological and behavioral responses associated with fear, aggression, and reward-seeking behavior. The hippocampus and cingulate cortex contribute to emotional regulation by modulating memory retrieval, emotional learning, and contextual understanding of emotional experiences.
- **Memory Formation and Consolidation**: The hippocampus is crucial for the formation and consolidation of declarative memories, including episodic memories of personal experiences and spatial navigation. It integrates information from cortical and subcortical regions to encode memories and retrieve stored information relevant to emotional contexts. Damage to the hippocampus can impair memory formation and retrieval, as seen in conditions such as amnesia and Alzheimer's disease.
- **Motivation and Reward**: The limbic system, particularly the hypothalamus and nucleus accumbens (part of the basal ganglia), regulates motivational states and reward-seeking behavior. The

hypothalamus integrates signals related to hunger, thirst, and sexual behavior, while the nucleus accumbens processes reward signals and reinforces behaviors associated with pleasurable experiences. Dysregulation of reward pathways in the limbic system can contribute to addictive behaviors and substance abuse disorders.

- **Olfaction (Sense of Smell)**: The limbic system, including the olfactory bulb and piriform cortex, processes olfactory information and links sensory stimuli with emotional responses and memory retrieval. Olfactory cues can evoke strong emotional reactions and trigger memories associated with specific scents, illustrating the limbic system's role in integrating sensory perception with emotional experiences.

Clinical Implications and Disorders

Disruptions in limbic system function are associated with various neurological and psychiatric disorders, including mood disorders (e.g., depression, anxiety), post-traumatic stress disorder (PTSD), Alzheimer's disease, and addiction. Dysregulation of emotional responses, memory deficits, and altered motivational states can result from structural damage, neurochemical imbalances, or pathological changes affecting limbic system structures.

Understanding the role of the limbic system in emotional processing, memory formation, and behavioral regulation provides insights into the mechanisms underlying neurological and psychiatric disorders. Therapeutic interventions targeting limbic system function, such as pharmacological treatments, cognitive-behavioral therapies, and neurostimulation techniques, aim to restore emotional regulation, enhance memory function, and alleviate symptoms associated with limbic system dysfunction.

In conclusion, the limbic system is a vital neural network involved in emotional processing, memory consolidation, motivation, and sensory integration. Its interconnected structures and regulatory functions contribute to adaptive behaviors, emotional responses, and cognitive processes essential for human survival and well-being. Enhancing our understanding of the limbic system provides insights into the neural mechanisms underlying emotional experiences, psychiatric disorders, and therapeutic strategies aimed at promoting emotional resilience and cognitive health across the lifespan.

4.3 Emotional Regulation and Dysregulation

Emotional regulation refers to the processes through which individuals manage and modulate their emotional experiences, expressions, and responses to achieve adaptive outcomes in various contexts. Effective emotional regulation involves the ability to monitor, evaluate, and modify emotional responses based on situational demands, personal goals, and social norms. Dysregulation of emotional responses can lead to difficulties in managing emotions, impairments in social functioning, and increased vulnerability to mental health disorders.

Components of Emotional Regulation

1. **Cognitive Reappraisal**: Cognitive reappraisal involves reframing the meaning or significance of emotional stimuli to alter emotional responses. This strategy relies on cognitive processes such as perspective-taking, reinterpretation of events, and generating

alternative explanations to modify the emotional impact of situations. By changing the appraisal of a situation, individuals can reduce negative emotional arousal and promote adaptive coping strategies.

2. **Expressive Suppression**: Expressive suppression involves inhibiting or concealing outward displays of emotional expressions, such as facial expressions, gestures, or vocalizations. While suppression can temporarily reduce visible signs of emotional arousal, it does not address underlying emotional experiences and may lead to increased physiological arousal or heightened emotional distress over time. Expressive suppression is often associated with reduced social engagement and interpersonal communication.

3. **Distraction and Attentional Control**: Distraction involves shifting attention away from emotional triggers or intrusive thoughts toward neutral or positive stimuli. By redirecting attentional focus, individuals can reduce emotional intensity and maintain cognitive control in challenging or distressing situations. Attentional control strategies enhance cognitive flexibility and resilience, promoting adaptive responses to emotional arousal.

4. **Response Modulation**: Response modulation involves regulating physiological arousal and behavioral responses associated with emotional experiences. Techniques such as deep breathing, progressive muscle relaxation, and mindfulness meditation can promote relaxation, reduce stress levels, and enhance self-regulation of emotional states. These techniques influence autonomic nervous system activity and promote physiological homeostasis during emotional arousal.

Development and Individual Differences

Emotional regulation skills develop throughout childhood and adolescence, influenced by genetic factors, environmental experiences, and social learning processes. Early attachment relationships, parenting styles, and peer interactions shape the development of emotion regulation strategies and adaptive coping mechanisms. Children learn to regulate emotions through modeling, reinforcement, and guided practice in managing emotional experiences within social contexts.

Individual differences in emotional regulation abilities contribute to variability in emotional resilience, stress tolerance, and mental health outcomes across individuals. Some individuals may demonstrate robust emotion regulation skills, effectively managing emotional challenges and maintaining psychological well-being, while others may experience difficulties in regulating emotions, leading to vulnerability to mood disorders, anxiety, or maladaptive coping behaviors.

Dysregulation and Mental Health Disorders

Dysregulation of emotional responses is a hallmark feature of various psychiatric disorders, including depression, anxiety disorders, post-traumatic stress disorder (PTSD), borderline personality disorder (BPD), and substance use disorders. Dysfunctional patterns of emotional regulation may involve heightened emotional reactivity, difficulty in modulating emotional intensity, or maladaptive coping strategies that exacerbate emotional distress.

Depression is characterized by persistent feelings of sadness, hopelessness, and diminished interest or pleasure in activities. Individuals with depression may experience difficulties in regulating negative emotions, maintaining motivation, and engaging in adaptive coping strategies to manage emotional distress.

Anxiety Disorders involve excessive worry, fear, or apprehension in response to perceived threats or uncertainties. Dysregulated emotional responses in anxiety disorders may manifest as heightened arousal, hypervigilance, and avoidance behaviors aimed at reducing perceived threat or discomfort.

PTSD develops in response to traumatic experiences and is characterized by intrusive memories, emotional numbing, and hyperarousal symptoms. Emotional dysregulation in PTSD may involve intense emotional reactions, flashbacks, and difficulty in modulating fear responses associated with traumatic memories.

Clinical Interventions and Treatment Approaches

Psychological interventions for emotional regulation disorders often include cognitive-behavioral therapies (CBT), dialectical behavior therapy (DBT), mindfulness-based interventions, and emotion-focused therapies. These approaches aim to enhance emotion regulation skills, promote adaptive coping strategies, and facilitate emotional processing and integration of traumatic experiences.

Pharmacological treatments may be prescribed to regulate neurotransmitter systems involved in emotional regulation, such as serotonin and norepinephrine, in individuals with mood disorders or anxiety-related conditions. Combined approaches involving psychotherapy and medication management can address both underlying emotional dysregulation and associated symptoms, promoting recovery and improving quality of life.

In conclusion, emotional regulation is essential for adaptive functioning and psychological well-being, involving cognitive, behavioral, and physiological processes that modulate emotional responses across different contexts. Dysregulation of emotional responses can contribute to the development and maintenance of psychiatric disorders, highlighting the importance of effective interventions aimed at enhancing emotion regulation skills, promoting resilience, and supporting mental health across the lifespan.

4.4 The Impact of Stress and Trauma on the Brain

Stress and trauma can profoundly impact brain structure and function, affecting neural circuits involved in emotional regulation, cognition, and physiological responses. Prolonged or severe stress can lead to structural changes in the brain, alter neurochemical balance, and dysregulate stress response systems, contributing to long-term psychological and physiological consequences.

Neurobiological Response to Stress

Stress activates the body's neuroendocrine system, including the hypothalamic-pituitary-adrenal (HPA) axis and sympathetic nervous system, to mobilize resources and prepare for adaptive responses to perceived threats. The hypothalamus releases corticotropin-releasing hormone (CRH), which stimulates the pituitary gland to release adrenocorticotropic hormone (ACTH). ACTH, in turn, triggers the release of cortisol from the adrenal glands, promoting physiological changes such as increased heart rate, elevated blood pressure, and heightened alertness.

Amygdala plays a crucial role in the initial detection and processing of threatening stimuli, initiating the activation of stress response systems and coordinating emotional responses. The amygdala's connections with the prefrontal cortex, hippocampus, and hypothalamus facilitate the integration of sensory information with emotional experiences and modulate fear responses and emotional arousal.

Prefrontal Cortex, particularly the ventromedial prefrontal cortex (VMPFC) and dorsolateral prefrontal cortex (DLPFC), regulates cognitive appraisal of stressors, inhibits inappropriate responses, and modulates emotional responses. Chronic stress can impair prefrontal cortex function, leading to deficits in decision-making, impulse control, and emotion regulation, exacerbating vulnerability to anxiety and mood disorders.

The hippocampus is involved in memory formation, spatial navigation, and the regulation of stress hormone secretion. Prolonged exposure to stress hormones, such as cortisol, can impair hippocampal function, reducing neurogenesis (formation of new neurons) and synaptic plasticity, which are essential for learning and memory processes. Hippocampal alterations may contribute to cognitive deficits observed in individuals exposed to chronic stress or trauma.

Impact of Trauma on Brain Structure and Function

Post-Traumatic Stress Disorder (PTSD) is a psychiatric disorder that can develop in response to exposure to traumatic events, such as combat, natural disasters, or interpersonal violence. PTSD is characterized by intrusive memories, hyperarousal, emotional numbing, and avoidance behaviors. Neuroimaging studies have identified structural and functional changes in brain regions implicated in emotional processing and stress regulation among individuals with PTSD.

Amygdala hyperactivation and enhanced threat response are commonly observed in individuals with PTSD, leading to heightened emotional reactivity and hypervigilance to potential threats. Altered connectivity between the amygdala and prefrontal cortex may impair emotion regulation and contribute to symptoms of anxiety and emotional dysregulation.

Hippocampal volume reduction is frequently reported in individuals with PTSD, reflecting stress-related neurotoxic effects on hippocampal neurons and compromised memory function. Diminished hippocampal volume may contribute to deficits in contextual memory retrieval and difficulties in distinguishing between past trauma and present safety cues.

Prefrontal Cortex dysfunction, characterized by reduced volume or hypoactivity, is associated with impairments in executive functions, such as decision-making, cognitive flexibility, and impulse control, observed in individuals with PTSD. Prefrontal cortical deficits contribute to difficulties in modulating emotional responses and inhibiting conditioned fear responses associated with trauma-related stimuli.

Neuroplasticity and Recovery

Despite the detrimental effects of stress and trauma on brain structure and function, the brain exhibits remarkable neuroplasticity—the ability to reorganize and adapt in response to experiences and environmental changes. Interventions such as trauma-focused therapies, cognitive-behavioral interventions, and pharmacological treatments aim to promote neural recovery, restore adaptive brain function, and alleviate symptoms associated with PTSD and related disorders.

Psychotherapeutic interventions, such as cognitive processing therapy (CPT) and eye movement desensitization and reprocessing (EMDR), target maladaptive cognitive and emotional responses to trauma, facilitating emotional processing and integration of traumatic memories. These therapies promote adaptive coping strategies, enhance resilience, and promote neural rewiring in brain regions involved in stress regulation and emotional processing.

Pharmacological treatments, such as selective serotonin reuptake inhibitors (SSRIs) and serotonin-norepinephrine reuptake inhibitors (SNRIs), may be prescribed to alleviate symptoms of depression and anxiety associated with PTSD and stabilize mood regulation. These medications modulate neurotransmitter systems implicated in stress response and emotional regulation, supporting recovery and improving the quality of life for individuals affected by trauma-related disorders.

In conclusion, stress and trauma exert profound effects on brain structure and function, influencing neural circuits involved in emotional regulation, cognition, and stress response. Understanding the neurobiological mechanisms underlying stress-related disorders, such as PTSD, informs therapeutic approaches aimed at promoting neural recovery, enhancing resilience, and restoring adaptive brain function in individuals exposed to traumatic experiences. Advances in neuroscience and clinical research continue to guide innovative treatments and interventions to support recovery and improve outcomes for individuals affected by stress-related disorders.

Chapter 5: Neuropsychology of Behavior

Neuropsychology explores the intricate relationship between brain function and behavior, examining how neurological processes influence cognitive abilities, emotional responses, and adaptive behaviors across diverse populations. By integrating insights from neuroscience, psychology, and clinical practice, researchers investigate how brain structure and function contribute to human behavior, personality traits, and psychological disorders.

Neural Substrates of Behavior

Behavioral neuroscience investigates the neural substrates underlying a wide range of behaviors, from basic sensory processing to complex cognitive functions and social interactions. Key brain regions implicated in behavior include:

1. **Prefrontal Cortex**: The prefrontal cortex, located at the front of the brain, plays a critical role in executive functions such as decision-making, planning, working memory, and impulse control. Damage or dysfunction in the prefrontal cortex can impair cognitive flexibility, emotional regulation, and social behavior, leading to deficits observed in conditions like attention-deficit hyperactivity disorder (ADHD) and frontal lobe syndrome.
2. **Limbic System**: The limbic system, comprising structures like the amygdala, hippocampus, and hypothalamus, regulates emotional responses, motivation, and memory processes. Emotional dysregulation, seen in mood disorders like depression or anxiety, may arise from abnormalities in limbic system function, affecting

emotional processing and behavioral responses to environmental stimuli.

3. **Basal Ganglia**: The basal ganglia are involved in motor control, habit formation, and reward processing. Dysfunctions in the basal ganglia can lead to movement disorders such as Parkinson's disease or Huntington's disease, characterized by impairments in motor coordination, involuntary movements, and changes in motivation or mood.

4. **Temporal Lobes**: The temporal lobes, including the hippocampus and adjacent areas, support auditory processing, language comprehension, and memory formation. Damage to the temporal lobes, as seen in temporal lobe epilepsy or traumatic brain injury, can result in deficits in auditory perception, language production, and episodic memory retrieval.

Cognitive Processes and Brain-Behavior Relationships

- **Attention and Perception**: Neuropsychological research examines how attentional processes, such as selective attention and sustained attention, are mediated by networks involving the frontal and parietal lobes. Perception, the interpretation of sensory information, relies on neural processing in sensory areas of the cortex, with integration and higher-order processing facilitated by association areas and the thalamus.

- **Memory Systems**: The study of memory encompasses various systems, including short-term memory (working memory) and long-term memory (declarative and procedural memory). The hippocampus, entorhinal cortex, and prefrontal cortex play essential roles in memory encoding, consolidation, and retrieval processes, influencing learning abilities and adaptive behaviors across the lifespan.

- **Language and Communication**: Language functions involve specialized neural circuits in the left hemisphere, including Broca's area for speech production and Wernicke's area for language comprehension. Neuropsychological assessment of language disorders, such as aphasia or dyslexia, provides insights into how disruptions in cortical language networks affect communication skills and linguistic processing.
- **Executive Functions**: Executive functions refer to higher-level cognitive processes responsible for goal-directed behavior, problem-solving, and self-regulation. The dorsolateral prefrontal cortex and anterior cingulate cortex coordinate executive functions by integrating information, monitoring performance, and adjusting behavior based on changing environmental demands.

Clinical Applications and Implications

Neuropsychological assessments and interventions are integral to diagnosing and treating neurological and psychiatric conditions that impact behavior and cognitive functioning. Clinical neuropsychologists utilize standardized tests, behavioral observations, and neuroimaging techniques to evaluate cognitive strengths and weaknesses, guide treatment planning, and monitor rehabilitation outcomes for individuals with brain injuries, neurodevelopmental disorders, or neurodegenerative diseases.

Understanding the neuropsychology of behavior informs therapeutic approaches aimed at promoting brain plasticity, enhancing adaptive behaviors, and improving the quality of life for individuals affected by neurological conditions. Interventions may include cognitive rehabilitation programs, behavioral therapies, pharmacological treatments, and supportive interventions tailored to address specific cognitive and emotional challenges associated with brain dysfunction.

In summary, the neuropsychology of behavior examines how brain structure and function influence cognitive processes, emotional responses, and behavioral outcomes across diverse populations. By elucidating the neural mechanisms underlying behavior, researchers and clinicians advance knowledge of brain-behavior relationships, inform diagnostic practices, and develop effective interventions to support cognitive health and well-being throughout the lifespan.

5.1 Motor Functions and Coordination

Motor functions and coordination are essential aspects of human behavior, relying on complex neural circuits and coordinated interactions between the brain, spinal cord, and peripheral nervous system. Understanding the neuropsychological basis of motor control elucidates how the brain orchestrates movements, maintains balance, and adapts motor behaviors in response to environmental demands and internal states.

Neural Substrates of Motor Control

Motor control involves the precise coordination of voluntary and involuntary movements through interconnected neural pathways and feedback mechanisms. Key brain regions and structures implicated in motor functions include:

1. **Primary Motor Cortex (M1)**: Located in the frontal lobe of the cerebral cortex, the primary motor cortex is responsible for initiating and executing voluntary movements. Neurons in M1 send signals through the corticospinal tract to the spinal cord, activating motor neurons that innervate muscles and control movement accuracy and force.

2. **Basal Ganglia**: The basal ganglia, including structures like the caudate nucleus, putamen, and globus pallidus, modulate motor planning, movement initiation, and motor learning. Dysfunctions in the basal ganglia can lead to movement disorders such as Parkinson's disease, characterized by tremors, rigidity, and bradykinesia (slowness of movement).

3. **Cerebellum**: The cerebellum, located at the base of the brain, coordinates motor coordination, balance, and posture through precise timing and modulation of muscle contractions. Damage to the cerebellum, as seen in cerebellar ataxia, disrupts smooth and coordinated movements, affecting gait stability and fine motor skills.

4. **Supplementary Motor Area (SMA) and Premotor Cortex**: The supplementary motor area and premotor cortex, situated in the frontal lobe, contribute to motor planning, sequencing of movements, and coordination of bilateral motor activities. These regions integrate sensory information and execute motor programs based on environmental cues and internal goals.

5. **Brainstem and Spinal Cord**: The brainstem, including structures like the medulla oblongata and pons, regulates basic motor functions such as breathing, heart rate, and reflexive movements. Descending motor pathways from the brainstem and spinal cord control voluntary and involuntary movements, supporting posture, locomotion, and reflex responses.

Motor Coordination and Control Mechanisms

- **Sensorimotor Integration**: Motor control relies on sensorimotor integration, the process of combining sensory feedback (proprioceptive, visual, and vestibular) with motor commands to adjust movements and maintain precision. Proprioceptive feedback from muscles, joints, and tendons informs the brain about limb position and muscle tension, facilitating coordinated movements and adjustments in response to external perturbations.
- **Motor Learning**: Motor learning involves acquiring and refining motor skills through practice and experience, mediated by neural plasticity and synaptic changes in motor pathways. Procedural memory systems, including the basal ganglia and cerebellum, consolidate motor patterns and automate repetitive movements over time, optimizing efficiency and accuracy.
- **Balance and Postural Control**: Balance and postural control are essential for maintaining stability during standing, walking, and dynamic activities. The cerebellum and vestibular system integrate sensory information about body position and movement to coordinate muscle responses and adjust the center of gravity, preventing falls and optimizing motor performance.

Clinical Implications and Motor Disorders

Motor disorders encompass a spectrum of neurological conditions characterized by impairments in movement control, coordination, and motor skills. Common motor disorders include:

1. **Parkinson's Disease**: Parkinson's disease results from degeneration of dopamine-producing neurons in the substantia nigra of the basal ganglia, leading to motor symptoms such as tremors, bradykinesia, rigidity, and postural instability.
2. **Cerebral Palsy**: Cerebral palsy is a group of motor disorders caused by brain damage or abnormal development, affecting movement, posture, and coordination. Individuals with cerebral palsy may experience spasticity, muscle weakness, and difficulties in fine motor control.
3. **Stroke**: Stroke occurs due to disruption of blood flow to the brain, resulting in motor deficits, paralysis, and impaired coordination on one side of the body (hemiparesis or hemiplegia). Rehabilitation focuses on restoring motor function through physical therapy and motor relearning techniques.
4. **Ataxia**: Ataxia refers to a lack of muscle coordination affecting movements such as walking, speech, and fine motor skills. Cerebellar ataxia, caused by damage to the cerebellum, disrupts balance, coordination, and motor planning.

Therapeutic Approaches and Rehabilitation

Neuropsychological interventions for motor disorders emphasize multidisciplinary approaches tailored to individual needs, focusing on improving motor function, enhancing independence, and optimizing quality of life. Therapeutic strategies may include:

1. **Physical Therapy**: Physical therapy aims to strengthen muscles, improve range of motion, and enhance motor control through exercises, stretching, and functional training.

2. **Occupational Therapy**: Occupational therapy addresses activities of daily living (ADLs) and fine motor skills, utilizing adaptive techniques and assistive devices to promote independence and functional mobility.
3. **Speech Therapy**: Speech therapy targets motor speech disorders (dysarthria) and language impairments, facilitating communication through articulation exercises and augmentative communication devices.
4. **Neuropsychological Rehabilitation**: Neuropsychological rehabilitation focuses on cognitive-behavioral strategies, compensatory techniques, and environmental modifications to support motor recovery and functional adaptation.

In conclusion, the neuropsychology of motor functions and coordination encompasses the study of neural mechanisms underlying movement control, sensorimotor integration, and motor learning. Understanding the neurobiological basis of motor disorders informs diagnostic assessment, therapeutic interventions, and rehabilitation strategies aimed at optimizing motor function and enhancing quality of life for individuals affected by neurological conditions impacting motor behavior.

5.2 Behavioral Inhibition and Impulsivity

Behavioral inhibition and impulsivity represent fundamental dimensions of human behavior, characterized by distinct cognitive and neural processes that modulate decision-making, self-control, and adaptive responses to environmental stimuli. Understanding these constructs from a neuropsychological perspective illuminates how neural circuits and neurotransmitter systems regulate inhibitory control and impulsivity, influencing behavior across different contexts and developmental stages.

Behavioral Inhibition

Behavioral inhibition refers to the ability to suppress or inhibit prepotent responses, delay gratification, and adaptively modulate behavior by internal goals or situational demands. This cognitive process involves executive functions mediated by frontal brain regions, particularly the prefrontal cortex (PFC), and neural networks responsible for response inhibition and self-regulation.

- **Prefrontal Cortex (PFC)**: The PFC, encompassing areas such as the dorsolateral prefrontal cortex (DLPFC) and ventromedial prefrontal cortex (VMPFC), plays a central role in executive functions, including inhibitory control, working memory, and cognitive flexibility. The DLPFC regulates goal-directed behaviors, planning, and decision-making, whereas the VMPFC integrates emotional and motivational information to guide behavioral responses.
- **Anterior Cingulate Cortex (ACC)**: The ACC monitors conflicts between competing stimuli or response options, facilitates error detection, and regulates cognitive control processes during decision-making tasks. Dysfunction in the ACC may impair adaptive adjustments in behavior and contribute to impulsivity or perseverative behaviors observed in psychiatric disorders.
- **Basal Ganglia**: The basal ganglia, including the striatum and nucleus accumbens, are involved in reward processing, habit formation, and motor responses. Inhibitory control mechanisms within the basal ganglia regulate the suppression of automatic or habitual behaviors in favor of goal-directed actions, influencing impulsivity and behavioral flexibility.

Impulsivity

Impulsivity refers to a tendency to act prematurely without foresight or consideration of consequences, often characterized by rapid decision-making, risk-taking behaviors, and difficulty inhibiting immediate responses. Impulsivity exists along a continuum, ranging from adaptive spontaneity to maladaptive behaviors associated with psychiatric disorders such as attention-deficit hyperactivity disorder (ADHD), substance use disorders, and borderline personality disorder (BPD).

- **Dopaminergic System**: Dopamine neurotransmission within mesolimbic and mesocortical pathways regulates reward processing, reinforcement learning, and motivational behaviors. Dysregulation of dopamine signaling, implicated in impulsivity and reward-seeking behaviors, may contribute to addictive behaviors and deficits in inhibitory control.
- **Serotonergic System**: Serotonin neurotransmission, primarily originating from the raphe nuclei in the brainstem, modulates mood regulation, emotional stability, and impulse control. Altered serotonin levels or receptor function are associated with impulsivity, aggression, and disorders characterized by poor impulse control, such as impulse control disorders and aggression-related behaviors.

Developmental and Clinical Perspectives

- **Developmental Trajectories**: Behavioral inhibition and impulsivity undergo developmental changes across childhood, adolescence, and adulthood, influenced by the maturation of prefrontal cortical regions and regulatory circuits. Early interventions promoting self-regulation and executive function skills may mitigate impulsivity and enhance adaptive behaviors in children and adolescents.

- **Clinical Implications**: Impulsivity is a core feature of several psychiatric disorders, including ADHD, substance use disorders, bipolar disorder, and personality disorders. Assessment tools such as neuropsychological tests, self-report measures, and behavioral observations are used to evaluate inhibitory control deficits and impulsivity in clinical populations.
- **Treatment Approaches**: Cognitive-behavioral therapies (CBT), dialectical behavior therapy (DBT), and mindfulness-based interventions target impulsivity by promoting cognitive restructuring, emotion regulation skills, and mindfulness practices. Pharmacological treatments, including stimulants for ADHD or selective serotonin reuptake inhibitors (SSRIs) for impulse control disorders, may complement psychotherapeutic approaches to enhance inhibitory control and reduce impulsivity.

Neurobiological Mechanisms and Neural Plasticity

Neuroscientific research emphasizes the role of neural plasticity in modulating inhibitory control and impulsivity, highlighting the brain's capacity to adapt and reorganize in response to environmental experiences and therapeutic interventions. Enhancing understanding of neurobiological mechanisms underlying behavioral inhibition and impulsivity informs innovative approaches to promote cognitive resilience, optimize self-regulation, and mitigate behavioral dysregulation across diverse populations.

In summary, behavioral inhibition and impulsivity represent dynamic constructs shaped by neurobiological processes, cognitive functions, and environmental influences. Advances in neuropsychology and neuroscience elucidate the neural substrates of inhibitory control, and impulsivity, and their implications for behavioral regulation, mental health, and therapeutic interventions aimed at enhancing self-control and adaptive decision-making skills.

5.3 Social Behavior and Interpersonal Relationships

Social behavior and interpersonal relationships are integral aspects of human interaction, shaped by complex cognitive, emotional, and neurobiological processes that facilitate communication, cooperation, and social bonding. Neuropsychological research explores the neural underpinnings of social behaviors, empathy, and social cognition, shedding light on how the brain processes social information, regulates emotional responses, and navigates interpersonal dynamics.

Neural Basis of Social Behavior

1. **Theory of Mind (ToM)**: Theory of Mind refers to the ability to attribute mental states, beliefs, and intentions to oneself and others, enabling individuals to understand and predict behavior based on internal mental states. ToM relies on neural networks involving the medial prefrontal cortex (mPFC), temporoparietal junction (TPJ), and superior temporal sulcus (STS), which integrate social cues and infer mental states during social interactions.
2. **Mirror Neuron System**: Mirror neurons, located in the premotor cortex and inferior parietal lobule, fire both when an individual

performs an action and observes others performing the same action. The mirror neuron system facilitates imitation, empathy, and understanding of others' actions and intentions, supporting social learning and interpersonal coordination.

3. **Limbic System and Emotion Regulation**: The limbic system, including the amygdala, hippocampus, and insula, modulates emotional responses and social behaviors through the integration of sensory information and the regulation of affective states. Emotional processing in social contexts involves reciprocal interactions between limbic structures and cortical regions implicated in cognitive appraisal and empathy.

Social Cognition and Emotional Intelligence

- **Empathy**: Empathy involves the ability to share and understand others' emotions, perspectives, and experiences, fostering interpersonal connection and prosocial behaviors. Neural correlates of empathy include activation in the anterior insula, anterior cingulate cortex (ACC), and mirror neuron system, which facilitate emotional resonance and perspective-taking during empathic responses.
- **Social Decision-Making**: Social decision-making encompasses processes such as trust, cooperation, reciprocity, and moral reasoning, influenced by neural circuits involved in reward processing, moral cognition, and social norms. The ventromedial prefrontal cortex (VMPFC), orbitofrontal cortex (OFC), and striatum integrate social and emotional information to guide adaptive behaviors in social contexts.
- **Attachment and Bonding**: Attachment behaviors, essential for forming and maintaining interpersonal relationships, are mediated

by oxytocinergic pathways originating from the hypothalamus and projecting to regions involved in social reward processing and affiliation, such as the nucleus accumbens and amygdala. Oxytocin facilitates bonding, trust, and social bonding behaviors across different relationship dynamics.

Developmental and Clinical Perspectives

- **Developmental Trajectories**: Social behaviors and interpersonal skills develop through interactions with caregivers, peers, and social environments, shaping neural circuits involved in social cognition and emotional regulation. Early childhood experiences influence the maturation of social brain networks and establish foundational skills for navigating social relationships across the lifespan.
- **Clinical Implications**: Impairments in social behavior and interpersonal relationships are evident in psychiatric disorders such as autism spectrum disorder (ASD), social anxiety disorder, and schizophrenia, characterized by deficits in social communication, social reciprocity, and emotional regulation. Neuropsychological assessments and interventions aim to enhance social skills, facilitate social integration, and improve the quality of life for individuals with social impairments.
- **Treatment Approaches**: Social skills training, cognitive-behavioral therapies (CBT), and social cognitive interventions target deficits in social cognition and interpersonal skills by promoting perspective-taking, emotion recognition, and adaptive social behaviors. Pharmacological treatments, such as oxytocin administration in ASD, may modulate social bonding and enhance social responsiveness in clinical populations.

Neurobiological Mechanisms and Social Plasticity

Neuroscientific investigations emphasize the role of neural plasticity in adapting to social experiences, modifying synaptic connections, and reorganizing neural circuits involved in social behavior and emotional processing. Social plasticity enables individuals to learn from social interactions, adjust social behaviors, and establish meaningful relationships based on shared experiences and emotional reciprocity.

In summary, social behavior and interpersonal relationships are shaped by neural processes that integrate cognitive, emotional, and social information to facilitate communication, empathy, and social bonding. Neuropsychological research advances our understanding of the neural substrates underlying social cognition, emotional intelligence, and social decision-making, informing therapeutic strategies to promote social competence, resilience, and well-being in diverse social contexts.

5.4 Neurodevelopmental and Behavioral Disorders

Neurodevelopmental and behavioral disorders encompass a spectrum of conditions characterized by atypical development of the nervous system, impairments in cognitive functioning, and behavioral disturbances that impact daily life and social interactions. Understanding the neurobiological underpinnings of these disorders informs diagnostic assessment, therapeutic interventions, and supportive strategies aimed at optimizing developmental outcomes and improving the quality of life for affected individuals.

Neurodevelopmental Disorders

1. **Autism Spectrum Disorder (ASD)**: ASD is a complex neurodevelopmental disorder characterized by persistent deficits in social communication and interaction, restricted interests, and repetitive behaviors. The etiology of ASD involves genetic factors, prenatal influences, and alterations in brain connectivity, particularly affecting regions implicated in social cognition (e.g., mirror neuron system, prefrontal cortex) and sensory processing (e.g., superior temporal sulcus, amygdala).
2. **Attention-Deficit/Hyperactivity Disorder (ADHD)**: ADHD is characterized by inattention, hyperactivity, and impulsivity, impairing academic performance, social relationships, and daily functioning. Neuroimaging studies implicate abnormalities in frontostriatal circuits, including the prefrontal cortex and basal ganglia, affecting executive functions, inhibitory control, and reward processing.
3. **Intellectual Disability (ID)**: Intellectual disability refers to limitations in intellectual functioning and adaptive behavior, manifesting during developmental periods and impacting cognitive abilities, communication skills, and adaptive functioning. Genetic syndromes, chromosomal abnormalities, and environmental factors contribute to variations in cognitive impairment and developmental trajectories.

Behavioral Disorders

1. **Conduct Disorder (CD)**: CD is characterized by persistent patterns of aggressive behavior, rule-breaking, and disregard for others' rights and societal norms. Neurobiological correlates

include dysfunction in amygdala-mediated emotional regulation, deficits in executive functions (e.g., impulsivity, decision-making) associated with prefrontal cortical abnormalities, and alterations in reward processing and empathy-related brain regions.

2. **Oppositional Defiant Disorder (ODD)**: ODD is characterized by defiant, disobedient, and hostile behaviors toward authority figures, without meeting the criteria for conduct disorder. Neural correlates involve impairments in emotion regulation, heightened amygdala reactivity to negative stimuli, and deficits in socioemotional processing mediated by prefrontal cortical regions and limbic system structures.

3. **Tourette syndrome (TS)**: TS is a neurodevelopmental disorder characterized by motor and vocal tics that emerge during childhood, affecting motor control and speech production. Alterations in cortico-striato-thalamo-cortical circuits, involving the basal ganglia and frontal cortex, contribute to tic expression, sensory hypersensitivity, and impulse control difficulties.

Diagnostic Assessment and Intervention

1. **Neuropsychological Assessment**: Diagnostic evaluations utilize standardized tests, clinical interviews, behavioral observations, and neuroimaging techniques to assess cognitive functioning, behavior patterns, and neural correlates of neurodevelopmental and behavioral disorders. Multidisciplinary teams collaborate to formulate comprehensive treatment plans tailored to individual needs.

2. **Therapeutic Approaches**: Treatment strategies for neurodevelopmental and behavioral disorders integrate behavioral interventions, psychoeducation, pharmacotherapy, and supportive therapies to address core symptoms, enhance adaptive skills, and

improve functional outcomes. Applied behavior analysis (ABA), social skills training, cognitive-behavioral therapy (CBT), and parent training programs are effective in promoting skill acquisition and behavioral modification.

3. **Pharmacological Interventions**: Pharmacotherapy targets specific symptom domains, such as attentional deficits in ADHD (e.g., stimulant medications) or mood dysregulation in mood disorders (e.g., selective serotonin reuptake inhibitors), to alleviate symptoms and improve behavioral management. Medication management is guided by individual response profiles, side-effect profiles, and ongoing monitoring of treatment efficacy.

Neurobiological Mechanisms and Developmental Plasticity

Neuroscientific research underscores the role of neural plasticity in modulating brain development, adaptive functioning, and response to therapeutic interventions in individuals with neurodevelopmental and behavioral disorders. Early interventions capitalize on neuroplasticity to promote neural reorganization, optimize developmental trajectories, and enhance cognitive resilience across diverse populations.

In summary, neurodevelopmental and behavioral disorders encompass a range of conditions characterized by disruptions in neurobiological processes, cognitive functioning, and behavioral regulation. Advances in neuropsychology and neuroscience inform diagnostic practices, therapeutic interventions, and supportive strategies aimed at fostering optimal developmental outcomes and improving the quality of life for individuals affected by these complex disorders.

Chapter 6: Cognitive and Emotional Disorders

Cognitive and emotional disorders encompass a diverse array of conditions characterized by disruptions in cognitive functioning, emotional regulation, and behavioral adaptation. These disorders impact perception, memory, decision-making, and affective responses, influencing individuals' daily lives, social interactions, and overall well-being. Understanding the neurobiological basis of cognitive and emotional disorders elucidates the underlying mechanisms, informs diagnostic assessment, and guides therapeutic interventions aimed at alleviating symptoms and improving cognitive resilience.

Neurobiological Underpinnings

1. **Major Depressive Disorder (MDD)**: MDD is a mood disorder characterized by persistent sadness, loss of interest or pleasure in activities, changes in appetite or sleep patterns, and feelings of worthlessness or guilt. Neurobiological research implicates dysregulation of monoaminergic neurotransmitter systems (e.g., serotonin, norepinephrine) and abnormalities in brain regions involved in emotional processing (e.g., amygdala, prefrontal cortex), contributing to mood disturbances and affective symptoms.
2. **Anxiety Disorders**: Anxiety disorders, including generalized anxiety disorder (GAD), panic disorder, and social anxiety disorder, involve excessive fear, worry, and avoidance behaviors that impair daily functioning. Dysfunctions in the amygdala-mediated fear response, altered GABAergic neurotransmission, and hyperactivity in limbic circuits contribute to heightened arousal, vigilance, and maladaptive responses to perceived threats.

3. **Schizophrenia Spectrum Disorders**: Schizophrenia spectrum disorders are characterized by disruptions in thinking, perception, emotions, and behavior, affecting cognitive processes such as attention, memory, and executive functions. Neurobiological abnormalities include dopamine dysregulation in mesolimbic and mesocortical pathways, NMDA receptor hypofunction, and structural abnormalities in cortical and subcortical regions, contributing to psychotic symptoms and cognitive impairments.

Cognitive Dysfunction and Disorders

1. **Alzheimer's Disease (AD)**: AD is a neurodegenerative disorder characterized by progressive cognitive decline, memory loss, and impairment in executive functions and visuospatial skills. Pathological hallmarks include beta-amyloid plaques and neurofibrillary tangles, leading to synaptic dysfunction, neuronal loss, and atrophy in cortical and hippocampal regions critical for memory encoding and retrieval.
2. **Mild Cognitive Impairment (MCI)**: MCI represents a transitional stage between normal cognitive aging and dementia, characterized by subtle memory deficits and cognitive impairment that do not significantly interfere with daily activities. Individuals with MCI have an increased risk of progressing to AD or other forms of dementia due to underlying neurodegenerative processes and cerebral pathology.

Diagnostic Assessment and Therapeutic Approaches

1. **Neuropsychological Assessment**: Diagnostic evaluations of cognitive and emotional disorders utilize comprehensive neuropsychological assessments, neuroimaging techniques (e.g., MRI, PET), and biomarker analysis to identify structural and functional abnormalities, monitor disease progression, and inform differential diagnosis.
2. **Pharmacological Interventions**: Pharmacotherapy targets specific neurotransmitter systems implicated in cognitive and emotional dysregulation, such as serotonin reuptake inhibitors (SSRIs) for mood disorders, antipsychotic medications for schizophrenia, and cholinesterase inhibitors for AD. Treatment regimens are tailored based on symptom severity, treatment response, and potential side effects.
3. **Cognitive Rehabilitation**: Cognitive rehabilitation programs aim to enhance cognitive functioning, promote compensatory strategies, and improve the quality of life for individuals with cognitive disorders. Interventions may include cognitive training exercises, memory enhancement techniques, and behavioral interventions to optimize functional independence and adaptive skills.

Neurobiological Mechanisms and Treatment Outcomes

Neuroscientific research highlights the role of neuroplasticity, neuroinflammation, and genetic factors in influencing treatment outcomes and disease progression in cognitive and emotional disorders. Therapeutic approaches targeting neuroprotection, synaptic remodeling, and neurotrophic support aim to mitigate neuronal damage, enhance neural resilience, and promote recovery of cognitive and emotional functions.

In summary, cognitive and emotional disorders encompass a spectrum of conditions characterized by disruptions in neurobiological processes, cognitive functioning, and emotional regulation. Advances in neuropsychology and neuroscience inform diagnostic practices, therapeutic interventions, and supportive strategies aimed at alleviating symptoms, improving cognitive resilience, and enhancing the quality of life for individuals affected by these complex disorders.

6.1 Neuropsychological Assessment and Diagnosis

Neuropsychological assessment is a specialized evaluation that examines the relationship between brain function and behavior, providing valuable insights into cognitive abilities, emotional functioning, and neurological integrity. This comprehensive approach integrates clinical observations, standardized tests, and neuroimaging findings to establish diagnoses, guide treatment planning, and monitor cognitive changes over time. Understanding the process of neuropsychological assessment illuminates its role in identifying neurocognitive disorders, elucidating underlying neurobiological mechanisms, and optimizing therapeutic interventions for individuals with neurological and psychiatric conditions.

Components of Neuropsychological Assessment

1. **Clinical Interview**: The assessment begins with a detailed clinical interview, where the neuropsychologist gathers information about the individual's medical history, developmental milestones, cognitive complaints, psychiatric symptoms, and functional

impairments. Family history, educational background, and psychosocial factors are also considered to contextualize cognitive and behavioral observations.

2. **Cognitive Testing**: Neuropsychological tests evaluate various cognitive domains, including attention, memory, executive functions, language, visuospatial skills, and processing speed. Standardized measures, such as the Mini-Mental State Examination (MMSE), Montreal Cognitive Assessment (MoCA), and Wechsler Adult Intelligence Scale (WAIS), assess cognitive strengths and weaknesses, providing quantitative data for comparison with normative samples.

3. **Emotional and Behavioral Assessment**: Behavioral observations and self-report measures assess emotional functioning, mood symptoms, personality traits, and adaptive behaviors. Rating scales, such as the Beck Depression Inventory (BDI), Hamilton Anxiety Rating Scale (HAM-A), and Behavior Rating Inventory of Executive Function (BRIEF), identify emotional disturbances and behavioral impairments impacting daily life and social interactions.

4. **Neuroimaging and Biomarker Analysis**: Neuroimaging techniques, including structural MRI, functional MRI (fMRI), positron emission tomography (PET), and diffusion tensor imaging (DTI), provide structural and functional insights into brain pathology, cerebral blood flow, white matter integrity, and neural connectivity. Biomarker analysis of cerebrospinal fluid (CSF) or blood samples may detect protein abnormalities associated with neurodegenerative diseases (e.g., beta-amyloid, tau proteins).

Diagnostic Utility and Clinical Applications

1. **Differential Diagnosis**: Neuropsychological assessment aids in differential diagnosis by distinguishing between neurocognitive

disorders (e.g., Alzheimer's disease, vascular dementia, frontotemporal dementia), psychiatric conditions (e.g., depression, schizophrenia), and functional impairments due to medical conditions (e.g., traumatic brain injury, stroke).

2. **Diagnostic Criteria and Classification Systems**: Diagnostic and Statistical Manual of Mental Disorders (DSM-5) criteria and International Classification of Diseases (ICD-10/ICD-11) guidelines provide standardized criteria for diagnosing neurocognitive disorders, psychiatric illnesses, and related conditions based on clinical presentation, cognitive testing results, and neuroimaging findings.

3. **Treatment Planning and Monitoring**: Neuropsychological assessment informs personalized treatment planning by identifying cognitive strengths and deficits, and guiding the selection of pharmacological interventions (e.g., cholinesterase inhibitors, antipsychotics) and psychosocial interventions (e.g., cognitive rehabilitation, psychotherapy). Longitudinal assessments monitor disease progression, therapeutic response, and functional outcomes to adjust treatment strategies and optimize patient care.

Ethical Considerations and Professional Standards

1. **Cultural Sensitivity**: Cultural factors, language barriers, and educational backgrounds influence test performance and interpretation, necessitating culturally competent assessment practices to ensure the validity and reliability of findings across diverse populations.

2. **Informed Consent**: Informed consent is obtained from individuals undergoing neuropsychological assessment, outlining the purpose, procedures, risks, and benefits of evaluation. Confidentiality and

privacy rights are upheld to safeguard sensitive health information and maintain trust between the clinician and patient.

3. **Interdisciplinary Collaboration**: Collaboration with neurologists, psychiatrists, neurosurgeons, and other healthcare professionals facilitates comprehensive care, multidisciplinary treatment planning, and integrated management of complex neurological and psychiatric conditions.

Advancing Research and Clinical Practice

Neuropsychological research advances the understanding of brain-behavior relationships, neural plasticity, and treatment outcomes in neurocognitive disorders. Innovations in technology, such as virtual reality simulations and computerized cognitive training programs, enhance assessment tools and therapeutic interventions, promoting cognitive rehabilitation and functional recovery in individuals with cognitive impairments.

In conclusion, neuropsychological assessment serves as a cornerstone in diagnosing neurocognitive and behavioral disorders, integrating clinical observations, cognitive testing, neuroimaging data, and psychosocial factors to inform treatment planning and improve the quality of life for individuals affected by neurological and psychiatric conditions. Ethical adherence to professional standards, cultural sensitivity, and interdisciplinary collaboration optimize diagnostic accuracy, therapeutic efficacy, and holistic patient care in clinical practice.

6.2 Cognitive Disorders: Dementia, Alzheimer's disease, and Others

Cognitive disorders encompass a spectrum of conditions characterized by impairments in cognitive abilities, memory, language, executive functions, and problem-solving skills. These disorders impact daily functioning, independence, and quality of life, reflecting underlying neurodegenerative processes, vascular pathology, or other neurological conditions. Understanding the clinical manifestations, neurobiological mechanisms, and diagnostic criteria of cognitive disorders, including dementia and Alzheimer's disease (AD), informs early detection, intervention strategies, and supportive care for affected individuals and their families.

Dementia: A General Overview

- **Definition and Clinical Features**: Dementia refers to a syndrome characterized by a progressive decline in cognitive function severe enough to interfere with daily activities and independent living. Common symptoms include memory loss, impaired judgment, language difficulties, disorientation, and changes in mood or behavior. Dementia syndromes encompass a range of etiologies and subtypes, each associated with distinct neuropathological changes and clinical presentations.
- **Neurobiological Underpinnings**: Neurodegenerative processes, cerebrovascular disease, and other pathological mechanisms contribute to dementia progression. Alzheimer's disease, vascular dementia, Lewy body dementia, frontotemporal dementia, and mixed dementia represent primary subtypes, each characterized by specific neuropathological features, such as beta-amyloid plaques

and neurofibrillary tangles in AD, cerebrovascular changes in vascular dementia, and protein aggregates in other forms.

Alzheimer's Disease (AD)

- **Epidemiology and Risk Factors**: AD is the most common cause of dementia, accounting for approximately 60-70% of cases. Advanced age is the primary risk factor, with incidence increasing sharply after age 65. Genetic factors (e.g., APOE ε4 allele), family history, cardiovascular risk factors (e.g., hypertension, diabetes), and lifestyle factors (e.g., physical inactivity, smoking) also influence disease susceptibility.
- **Pathophysiology**: AD is characterized by progressive neurodegeneration, involving the accumulation of beta-amyloid plaques and neurofibrillary tangles composed of hyperphosphorylated tau protein. Beta-amyloid deposition disrupts synaptic function and promotes neuronal toxicity, while tau pathology correlates with neurofibrillary degeneration and cognitive decline, particularly affecting memory and executive functions.
- **Clinical Stages and Diagnosis**: AD progresses through mild cognitive impairment (MCI) to mild, moderate, and severe stages of dementia, marked by increasing cognitive deficits and functional impairments. Diagnosis relies on clinical assessment, neuropsychological testing, neuroimaging (e.g., MRI, PET scans), and biomarker analysis (e.g., CSF analysis of beta-amyloid and tau proteins) to differentiate AD from other dementias and neurocognitive disorders.

Other Cognitive Disorders

- **Vascular Dementia**: Vascular dementia results from cerebrovascular disease, including stroke, ischemic lesions, and small vessel disease, leading to cognitive impairments in attention, executive functions, and motor skills. Risk factors include hypertension, diabetes, hyperlipidemia, and cardiovascular disease, contributing to vascular pathology and white matter changes observed on neuroimaging.
- **Lewy Body Dementia (LBD)**: LBD is characterized by the presence of alpha-synuclein aggregates (Lewy bodies) in cortical and subcortical brain regions, causing fluctuations in cognition, visual hallucinations, parkinsonism, and REM sleep behavior disorder. LBD shares clinical features with Parkinson's disease dementia and overlaps with Alzheimer's pathology, presenting diagnostic challenges due to variable symptomatology.
- **Frontotemporal Dementia (FTD)**: FTD encompasses a group of disorders characterized by progressive atrophy of the frontal and temporal lobes, affecting behavior, personality, language, and executive functions. Subtypes include behavioral variant FTD, semantic variant primary progressive aphasia (PPA), and non-fluent variant PPA, each associated with distinct clinical profiles and neuropathological changes.

Treatment and Management

- **Pharmacological Interventions**: Pharmacotherapy for AD includes cholinesterase inhibitors (e.g., donepezil, rivastigmine) and NMDA receptor antagonists (e.g., memantine), targeting symptomatic relief and cognitive stabilization by enhancing neurotransmission and modulating glutamatergic pathways. Treatment efficacy varies based on disease stage and individual response.

- **Non-Pharmacological Approaches**: Non-pharmacological interventions include cognitive rehabilitation, behavioral therapy, caregiver education, and psychosocial support programs. These interventions promote functional independence, enhance quality of life, and alleviate caregiver burden through structured activities, memory aids, and adaptive strategies tailored to individual needs.

Future Directions and Research Advances

Advances in neuroimaging biomarkers, genetic testing, and precision medicine hold promise for early detection, personalized treatment strategies, and disease-modifying therapies targeting underlying pathophysiological mechanisms in cognitive disorders. Research efforts focus on neuroprotection, synaptic repair, and cognitive enhancement to optimize therapeutic outcomes and improve long-term prognosis for individuals affected by dementia and related conditions.

In conclusion, cognitive disorders encompass a spectrum of neurodegenerative and vascular conditions characterized by progressive cognitive decline, memory loss, and functional impairments. A comprehensive understanding of disease mechanisms, diagnostic criteria, and treatment modalities informs clinical practice, promotes early intervention, and enhances the quality of life for individuals living with dementia, Alzheimer's disease, and other cognitive disorders.

6.3 Mood Disorders: Depression, Bipolar Disorder, and Anxiety

Mood disorders encompass a broad category of mental health conditions characterized by disturbances in mood regulation, emotional processing, and affective states. These disorders significantly impact individuals' emotional well-being, cognitive functioning, social relationships, and overall quality of life. Understanding the clinical manifestations, neurobiological underpinnings, and treatment approaches for mood disorders, including depression, bipolar disorder, and anxiety disorders, is essential for effective diagnosis, intervention, and supportive care.

Depression (Major Depressive Disorder)

- **Definition and Clinical Features**: Major Depressive Disorder (MDD) is a pervasive mood disorder characterized by persistent feelings of sadness, loss of interest or pleasure in activities once enjoyed (anhedonia), changes in appetite or weight, sleep disturbances, fatigue, feelings of worthlessness or guilt, and suicidal thoughts or behaviors. Symptoms must persist for at least two weeks to meet diagnostic criteria.
- **Neurobiological Mechanisms**: Neurotransmitter dysregulation, particularly involving serotonin, norepinephrine, and dopamine systems, plays a critical role in MDD pathophysiology. Dysfunction in neural circuits, including the prefrontal cortex, amygdala, and hippocampus, contributes to emotional dysregulation, altered stress responses, and impairments in reward processing and executive functions.
- **Diagnosis and Assessment**: Diagnosis of MDD relies on clinical assessment, psychiatric interviews, and standardized diagnostic

criteria outlined in the Diagnostic and Statistical Manual of Mental Disorders (DSM-5). Rating scales, such as the Beck Depression Inventory (BDI) and Hamilton Rating Scale for Depression (HAM-D), quantify symptom severity and monitor treatment response.

Bipolar Disorder

- **Definition and Clinical Subtypes**: Bipolar disorder is characterized by recurrent episodes of mood disturbance, including manic episodes (elevated mood, grandiosity, increased energy) and depressive episodes (similar to MDD symptoms). Bipolar I disorder involves manic episodes with or without depressive episodes, while Bipolar II disorder features hypomanic episodes and depressive episodes.
- **Neurobiological Underpinnings**: Dysregulation of neurotransmitter systems, including dopamine, serotonin, and norepinephrine, contributes to mood instability and cycling between manic and depressive states. Structural and functional abnormalities in brain regions, such as the prefrontal cortex, striatum, and limbic system, impact emotional regulation, impulse control, and reward processing.
- **Diagnosis and Assessment**: Diagnosis of bipolar disorder involves clinical evaluation, mood symptom monitoring over time, and consideration of family history and genetic predisposition. The Mood Disorders Questionnaire (MDQ) and Young Mania Rating Scale (YMRS) assess manic symptoms, while mood rating scales and structured interviews aid in differential diagnosis and treatment planning.

Anxiety Disorders

- **Types and Clinical Features**: Anxiety disorders encompass a spectrum of conditions characterized by excessive fear, worry, and avoidance behaviors that impair daily functioning and social interactions. Common types include Generalized Anxiety Disorder (GAD), Panic Disorder, Social Anxiety Disorder (SAD), and specific phobias. Symptoms may include restlessness, irritability, muscle tension, insomnia, and panic attacks.
- **Neurobiological Mechanisms**: Dysregulation of the amygdala-mediated fear response, altered GABAergic neurotransmission, and hyperactivity in corticolimbic circuits (e.g., anterior cingulate cortex, insula) contribute to heightened arousal, hypervigilance, and maladaptive responses to perceived threats. Neuroimaging studies demonstrate structural and functional changes in brain regions involved in fear conditioning and emotional processing.
- **Diagnosis and Assessment**: Diagnosis of anxiety disorders involves clinical evaluation, self-report measures (e.g., Generalized Anxiety Disorder 7-item scale, GAD-7), and structured interviews to assess symptom severity, functional impairment, and comorbid conditions. Differential diagnosis considers specific phobias, obsessive-compulsive disorder (OCD), and post-traumatic stress disorder (PTSD), based on symptom duration and clinical presentation.

Treatment Approaches

- **Pharmacological Interventions**: Antidepressants, such as selective serotonin reuptake inhibitors (SSRIs) and serotonin-norepinephrine reuptake inhibitors (SNRIs), are first-line treatments for depression and anxiety disorders. Mood stabilizers (e.g., lithium, anticonvulsants) and atypical antipsychotics manage manic symptoms in bipolar disorder, targeting neurotransmitter imbalances and stabilizing mood fluctuations.

- **Psychotherapy**: Cognitive-behavioral therapy (CBT), interpersonal therapy (IPT), and mindfulness-based interventions address cognitive distortions, behavioral patterns, and emotional regulation strategies in mood disorders and anxiety disorders. Therapy modalities promote adaptive coping skills, resilience, and symptom management across different phases of illness.

Integrated Care and Holistic Approaches

Collaborative care models integrate psychiatric treatment, psychotherapy, and psychosocial support to address multidimensional aspects of mood disorders and anxiety disorders. Holistic approaches encompass lifestyle modifications (e.g., exercise, nutrition), stress management techniques (e.g., relaxation exercises, mindfulness meditation), and peer support groups to enhance treatment adherence and overall well-being.

Future Directions in Research and Treatment

Advancements in neuroimaging, genetics, and neurobiology elucidate biomarkers of treatment response, disease progression, and personalized medicine approaches in mood disorders and anxiety disorders. Research initiatives focus on neuroprotective strategies, targeted interventions, and digital health technologies to optimize therapeutic outcomes and improve the long-term prognosis for individuals affected by these prevalent mental health conditions.

In summary, mood disorders, including depression, bipolar disorder, and anxiety disorders, present complex challenges in clinical practice, requiring comprehensive assessment, evidence-based interventions, and holistic care approaches to promote recovery, resilience, and quality of life for individuals and their families. Understanding the neurobiological underpinnings and treatment modalities advances therapeutic strategies and enhances outcomes in managing these debilitating mental health disorders.

6.4 Psychotic Disorders: Schizophrenia and Other Psychoses

Psychotic disorders constitute a group of severe mental illnesses characterized by disturbances in perception, thought processes, emotions, and behavior, leading to profound disruptions in cognitive functioning and daily life. Among these disorders, schizophrenia represents the prototypical condition, marked by hallucinations, delusions, disorganized thinking, and impaired social functioning. Understanding the clinical manifestations, neurobiological mechanisms, and treatment approaches for schizophrenia and other psychoses is crucial for effective diagnosis, intervention, and supportive care.

Schizophrenia: Overview and Clinical Features

- **Definition and Diagnostic Criteria**: Schizophrenia is a chronic and severe psychiatric disorder characterized by a combination of positive symptoms (hallucinations, delusions, disorganized speech or behavior) and negative symptoms (social withdrawal, diminished emotional expression, avolition). Symptoms must persist for at least six months and significantly impair social or occupational functioning to meet diagnostic criteria outlined in the Diagnostic and Statistical Manual of Mental Disorders (DSM-5).

- **Neurobiological Underpinnings**: The neurobiology of schizophrenia involves complex interactions among genetic predisposition, neurotransmitter dysregulation (particularly dopamine and glutamate), structural brain abnormalities (e.g., enlarged ventricles, reduced gray matter volume), and altered neural connectivity in cortical and subcortical regions. Dopamine hypothesis posits hyperactivity of mesolimbic dopamine pathways contributing to positive symptoms, while hypoactivity in mesocortical pathways underlies negative symptoms and cognitive deficits.
- **Clinical Subtypes and Disease Course**: Schizophrenia presents with heterogeneous clinical subtypes, including paranoid, disorganized, catatonic, residual, and undifferentiated types, each characterized by varying symptom profiles and disease trajectories. Early-onset schizophrenia may manifest in adolescence or early adulthood, whereas late-onset schizophrenia occurs later in life, often associated with cognitive decline and functional impairment.

Other Psychotic Disorders

- **Schizoaffective Disorder**: Schizoaffective disorder combines features of schizophrenia (psychotic symptoms) and mood disorders (mania or depression), presenting with alternating episodes of psychosis and mood disturbances. Diagnosis involves careful differentiation from primary mood disorders and schizophrenia spectrum disorders based on temporal patterns and symptom severity.

- **Brief Psychotic Disorder**: Brief psychotic disorder is characterized by sudden onset of psychotic symptoms (e.g., hallucinations, delusions, disorganized behavior) lasting at least one day but less than one month, typically triggered by acute stressors or traumatic events. Symptoms may remit spontaneously or require brief hospitalization for stabilization and supportive care.
- **Delusional Disorder**: Delusional disorder involves fixed, false beliefs (delusions) that persist for at least one month without prominent hallucinations, disorganized thinking, or grossly impaired functioning. Subtypes include persecutory, grandiose, jealous, erotomanic, and somatic delusions, impacting interpersonal relationships and daily functioning while maintaining relative preservation of cognitive abilities.

Treatment Approaches

- **Pharmacological Interventions**: Antipsychotic medications, such as first-generation (typical) and second-generation (atypical) antipsychotics, are cornerstone treatments for schizophrenia and psychotic disorders. Antipsychotics block dopamine D2 receptors, alleviate positive symptoms and modulate serotonin and glutamate neurotransmission to improve cognitive function and reduce relapse rates. Treatment adherence and choice of medication are tailored based on symptom severity, side effect profiles, and individual response.
- **Psychosocial Interventions**: Psychosocial interventions complement pharmacotherapy by addressing social skills deficits,

enhancing adaptive coping strategies, promoting medication adherence, and improving functional outcomes in schizophrenia and psychotic disorders. Cognitive-behavioral therapy (CBT), supportive therapy, family psychoeducation, vocational rehabilitation, and assertive community treatment (ACT) facilitate recovery, reduce hospitalizations, and enhance quality of life.

Holistic Care and Long-Term Management

Integrated care models emphasize holistic approaches to managing schizophrenia and psychotic disorders, incorporating multidisciplinary teams (e.g., psychiatrists, psychologists, and social workers) to provide comprehensive assessment, treatment planning, and ongoing support. Collaborative efforts focus on early intervention, crisis intervention, relapse prevention, and addressing comorbid medical and psychiatric conditions to optimize long-term outcomes and promote recovery.

Advances in Research and Future Directions

Advancements in neuroimaging, genetics, and neurobiology advance understanding of schizophrenia's etiology, disease progression, and treatment response variability. Research initiatives explore novel therapeutic targets (e.g., glutamatergic modulators, neuroprotective agents), personalized medicine approaches, and digital health interventions to enhance treatment efficacy, minimize side effects, and improve functional outcomes for individuals living with psychotic disorders.

In conclusion, psychotic disorders, including schizophrenia and related psychoses, pose significant challenges in clinical practice, requiring comprehensive evaluation, evidence-based interventions, and compassionate care to address complex symptomatology, functional impairment, and psychosocial impact. Collaborative efforts in research and clinical care aim to optimize treatment strategies, promote recovery, and enhance the quality of life for individuals affected by these debilitating psychiatric conditions.

Chapter 7: Neuropsychological Interventions and Therapies

Neuropsychological interventions and therapies encompass a diverse array of approaches aimed at addressing cognitive, emotional, and behavioral impairments resulting from neurological conditions, brain injuries, or psychiatric disorders. These interventions are tailored to individual needs, focusing on improvingcognitive functioning, improving emotional regulation, and promoting adaptive behaviors to optimize overall quality of life. Understanding the principles, methodologies, and clinical applications of neuropsychological interventions is essential for clinicians, researchers, and caregivers involved in rehabilitation and treatment planning.

Cognitive Rehabilitation

- **Definition and Goals**: Cognitive rehabilitation aims to restore or enhance cognitive abilities, including attention, memory, executive functions, and problem-solving skills, through structured and targeted interventions. Principles of neuroplasticity guide treatment strategies, emphasizing the brain's capacity to reorganize and adapt following injury or disease.
- **Techniques and Approaches**: Cognitive rehabilitation employs evidence-based techniques such as cognitive training, compensatory strategies, and environmental modifications to improve cognitive processing speed, accuracy, and efficiency. Task-specific training, computer-assisted programs, and mnemonic strategies enhance learning, memory consolidation, and functional independence in daily activities.

- **Clinical Applications**: Cognitive rehabilitation is integral in managing cognitive deficits associated with traumatic brain injury (TBI), stroke, neurodegenerative diseases (e.g., Alzheimer's disease), and neurological disorders (e.g., multiple sclerosis). Individualized treatment plans address cognitive strengths and weaknesses, adapting interventions based on cognitive profiles and rehabilitation goals.

Behavioral and Emotional Interventions

- **Definition and Objectives**: Behavioral and emotional interventions focus on modifying maladaptive behaviors, managing emotional dysregulation, and improving social skills in individuals with neurological or psychiatric conditions. Therapeutic techniques promote self-awareness, emotional expression, and interpersonal communication to enhance psychosocial functioning.
- **Therapeutic Approaches**: Cognitive-behavioral therapy (CBT), dialectical behavior therapy (DBT), and mindfulness-based interventions address cognitive distortions, negative thought patterns, and emotional reactivity associated with mood disorders, anxiety disorders, and psychotic disorders. Behavioral interventions utilize reinforcement techniques, social skills training, and contingency management to promote adaptive behaviors and reduce disruptive symptoms.
- **Clinical Applications**: Behavioral and emotional interventions are employed in treating behavioral disturbances (e.g., aggression, impulsivity) in traumatic brain injury, managing psychiatric symptoms (e.g., depression, anxiety) in neurodegenerative diseases, and facilitating emotional regulation in autism spectrum

disorders. Multidisciplinary teams collaborate to implement personalized interventions tailored to individual needs and treatment goals.

Psychosocial Support and Rehabilitation

- **Definition and Scope**: Psychosocial support encompasses comprehensive interventions designed to address psychological, social, and environmental factors influencing recovery and adaptation to neurological or psychiatric conditions. Rehabilitation programs foster community integration, vocational rehabilitation, and caregiver support to enhance functional outcomes and quality of life.
- **Intervention Strategies**: Psychosocial interventions include psychoeducation, family therapy, vocational rehabilitation, and peer support groups to empower individuals and caregivers with knowledge, coping skills, and social resources. Case management services coordinate care, facilitate access to community resources, and promote continuity of care across treatment settings.
- **Clinical Applications**: Psychosocial support and rehabilitation are integral components of chronic disease management in neurological disorders (e.g., Parkinson's disease, multiple sclerosis), promoting adaptive coping strategies, enhancing caregiver resilience, and mitigating psychosocial stressors impacting patient and family well-being.

Emerging Trends and Future Directions

Advancements in technology, virtual reality, and telehealth platforms expand access to neuropsychological interventions, facilitating remote assessment, treatment delivery, and caregiver training. Research initiatives focus on personalized medicine approaches, neurostimulation techniques (e.g., transcranial magnetic stimulation, deep brain stimulation), and neurorehabilitation strategies to optimize treatment efficacy, neuroplasticity, and long-term functional outcomes.

In conclusion, neuropsychological interventions and therapies encompass a continuum of evidence-based approaches aimed at addressing cognitive, emotional, and behavioral impairments in neurological and psychiatric populations. Collaborative efforts among clinicians, researchers, and caregivers promote innovative treatment strategies, enhance therapeutic outcomes, and improve the quality of life for individuals affected by brain injury, neurodegenerative diseases, and mental health disorders. Integrating principles of neuroplasticity, personalized care, and psychosocial support facilitates holistic rehabilitation, fostering resilience and adaptive functioning in diverse clinical settings.

7.1 Rehabilitation Techniques and Strategies

Rehabilitation techniques and strategies in neuropsychology encompass a spectrum of therapeutic approaches aimed at enhancing cognitive, emotional, and behavioral functioning in individuals affected by neurological conditions, brain injuries, or psychiatric disorders. These interventions are tailored to address specific impairments and functional limitations, promoting recovery, adaptation, and improved quality of life. Understanding the diverse methodologies and clinical applications of rehabilitation techniques is crucial for healthcare professionals, therapists, and caregivers involved in the rehabilitation process.

Cognitive Rehabilitation

Cognitive rehabilitation focuses on improving cognitive abilities such as attention, memory, executive functions, and problem-solving skills. Techniques include:

1. **Cognitive Training**: Structured exercises and tasks designed to target specific cognitive deficits, such as attentional drills, memory exercises, and reasoning tasks. Cognitive training programs are tailored to individual needs, emphasizing repetition, task complexity, and gradual progression to enhance cognitive processing.
2. **Compensatory Strategies**: Adaptive techniques and tools to compensate for cognitive impairments and facilitate everyday functioning. Examples include using memory aids (e.g., calendars, organizers), visual cues, and environmental modifications (e.g., reducing distractions) to support cognitive tasks and promote independence.
3. **Task-Specific Practice**: Real-world simulations and functional activities to practice skills in contexts relevant to daily life. Occupational therapists and rehabilitation specialists integrate task-specific training to improve functional outcomes, such as cooking, managing finances, and using public transportation.

Behavioral Interventions

Behavioral interventions target maladaptive behaviors, emotional dysregulation, and social skills deficits in individuals with neurological or psychiatric conditions:

1. **Behavioral Modification**: Techniques such as reinforcement strategies, contingency management, and token economies to promote adaptive behaviors and reduce problematic behaviors (e.g., aggression, impulsivity). Behavior therapists collaborate with individuals and caregivers to implement behavior plans tailored to specific goals.
2. **Social Skills Training**: Structured interventions to improve interpersonal communication, assertiveness, and social interactions. Role-playing exercises, group therapy sessions, and peer support facilitate skill acquisition, self-confidence, and community integration for individuals with social deficits.
3. **Cognitive-Behavioral Therapy (CBT)**: Psychotherapeutic approach targeting cognitive distortions, negative thought patterns, and emotional regulation difficulties. CBT techniques include cognitive restructuring, relaxation techniques, and exposure therapy to address anxiety disorders, depression, and post-traumatic stress disorder (PTSD).

Psychosocial Support

Psychosocial support interventions encompass holistic approaches to address psychological, social, and environmental factors impacting rehabilitation and recovery:

1. **Psychoeducation**: Providing information and education to individuals and families about the nature of their condition, treatment options, and coping strategies. Psychoeducational programs empower individuals with knowledge, promote treatment adherence, and enhance self-management skills.
2. **Family Therapy**: Counseling and support for families to improve communication, reduce caregiver stress, and enhance family dynamics. Family therapists collaborate with caregivers to develop coping strategies, promote patient independence, and address caregiving challenges.
3. **Vocational Rehabilitation**: Programs and services to support individuals in returning to work or pursuing meaningful employment. Vocational counselors assess skills, provide job training, and facilitate workplace accommodations to promote vocational success and financial independence.

Integrative Approaches

1. **Multidisciplinary Collaboration**: Team-based approaches involving neurologists, psychologists, occupational therapists, speech-language pathologists, and social workers to coordinate comprehensive care. Multidisciplinary teams collaborate on treatment planning, goal setting, and progress monitoring to optimize rehabilitation outcomes.
2. **Technology-Assisted Interventions**: Integration of technology, such as virtual reality (VR), computerized cognitive training programs, and telehealth platforms, to enhance accessibility, engagement, and effectiveness of rehabilitation interventions. Virtual environments and digital tools simulate real-life scenarios, provide immediate feedback, and facilitate remote monitoring of progress.

Future Directions

Advancements in neuroscience, neuroimaging, and personalized medicine continue to shape the field of neuropsychological rehabilitation. Research focuses on neuroplasticity, biomarker identification, and innovative interventions (e.g., brain stimulation techniques, neurofeedback) to enhance recovery trajectories, tailor treatment approaches, and improve long-term outcomes for individuals with neurological and psychiatric conditions.

In conclusion, rehabilitation techniques and strategies in neuropsychology emphasize evidence-based interventions tailored to individual needs and functional goals. Integrating cognitive, behavioral, and psychosocial approaches promotes holistic rehabilitation, enhances adaptive functioning, and fosters resilience in individuals facing neurological challenges. Collaborative efforts among healthcare professionals, researchers, and caregivers drive innovation, optimize treatment outcomes, and improve the quality of life for individuals on their rehabilitation journey.

7.2 Cognitive Behavioral Therapy (CBT) and Other Therapeutic Approaches

Cognitive Behavioral Therapy (CBT) and other therapeutic approaches represent cornerstone interventions in psychological and behavioral health, addressing a wide range of mental health conditions through structured, goal-oriented techniques. These therapies are grounded in evidence-based practices and tailored to individual needs, promoting cognitive restructuring, behavior modification, and emotional regulation to facilitate lasting change and improved well-being.

Cognitive Behavioral Therapy (CBT)

Definition and Principles: CBT is a widely recognized psychotherapeutic approach that combines cognitive and behavioral strategies to treat various mental health disorders. It operates on the premise that dysfunctional thoughts and behaviors contribute to psychological distress, and by modifying these patterns, individuals can improve their emotional functioning and coping skills.

Techniques and Applications: CBT techniques include:

- **Cognitive Restructuring**: Identifying and challenging negative thought patterns (cognitive distortions) that contribute to anxiety, depression, or other disorders. This process involves examining evidence for and against these thoughts and developing more balanced and realistic alternatives.
- **Behavioral Activation**: Encouraging engagement in positive and rewarding activities to counteract withdrawal and depressive symptoms. Behavioral activation helps individuals reconnect with enjoyable activities and increase motivation.
- **Exposure Therapy**: Gradual and systematic exposure to feared or avoided situations, stimuli, or memories to reduce anxiety responses. Exposure therapy is effective for phobias, post-traumatic stress disorder (PTSD), and obsessive-compulsive disorder (OCD), helping individuals confront and manage their fears.
- **Skills Training**: Teaching practical skills such as problem-solving, assertiveness, and relaxation techniques to enhance coping abilities and manage stressors effectively.

- **Clinical Effectiveness**: CBT is extensively researched and demonstrated effective in treating depression, anxiety disorders (e.g., generalized anxiety disorder, social anxiety disorder), PTSD, OCD, eating disorders, and substance abuse. It is typically delivered in a structured format over a defined number of sessions, promoting symptom relief and long-term recovery.

Other Therapeutic Approaches

1. **Dialectical Behavior Therapy (DBT)**: Originally developed for borderline personality disorder (BPD), DBT integrates cognitive-behavioral techniques with mindfulness practices. It emphasizes acceptance of emotions, interpersonal effectiveness, distress tolerance, and emotion regulation skills. DBT is effective in treating BPD, suicidal behaviors, and chronic emotional dysregulation.
2. **Acceptance and Commitment Therapy (ACT)**: ACT focuses on the acceptance of negative thoughts and feelings rather than their elimination, promoting mindfulness, values clarification, and committed action toward meaningful life goals. ACT is effective for anxiety disorders, depression, chronic pain, and psychosis.
3. **Mindfulness-Based Interventions**: Derived from mindfulness-based stress reduction (MBSR) and mindfulness-based cognitive therapy (MBCT), these interventions cultivate present-moment awareness, acceptance, and non-judgmental attitudes toward thoughts and emotions. Mindfulness practices reduce stress, enhance emotional resilience, and prevent relapse into depression and anxiety.
4. **Interpersonal Therapy (IPT)**: IPT addresses interpersonal conflicts, role transitions, grief, and social isolation by improving communication skills, resolving relationship issues, and enhancing

social support networks. IPT is effective for depression, eating disorders, and adjustment disorders.

Integrative Approaches and Future Directions

1. **Integrative Therapy Models**: Many therapeutic approaches integrate elements from different modalities to tailor treatment to individual needs and complexities of psychological disorders. Integrative approaches enhance treatment outcomes by combining cognitive restructuring, behavioral interventions, mindfulness practices, and interpersonal skills training.
2. **Technology and Therapeutic Innovation**: Digital health platforms, mobile applications, and teletherapy services expand access to therapeutic interventions, facilitate self-monitoring, and deliver personalized treatment plans. Virtual reality (VR) and augmented reality (AR) are emerging tools for exposure therapy and social skills training, providing immersive environments for therapeutic practice.
3. **Advancements in Neuroscience**: Ongoing neuroscience research explores neurobiological mechanisms underlying therapeutic change, biomarkers of treatment response, and personalized interventions based on genetic, neuroimaging, and physiological data. These advancements inform targeted therapies and optimize treatment outcomes for diverse populations.

In conclusion, Cognitive Behavioral Therapy (CBT) and other therapeutic approaches play pivotal roles in treating mental health disorders by addressing cognitive, emotional, and behavioral patterns that contribute to psychological distress. These evidence-based interventions promote symptom relief, enhance coping skills, and improve overall quality of life, underscoring their significance in contemporary mental health care practices. Collaborative efforts among clinicians, researchers, and stakeholders continue to refine therapeutic strategies, integrate innovative technologies, and advance knowledge in optimizing psychological well-being and treatment efficacy across diverse populations.

7.3 Pharmacological Interventions

Pharmacological interventions are a cornerstone in the treatment of numerous neurological and psychiatric disorders, providing symptom relief and improving the quality of life for many patients. These interventions are based on a comprehensive understanding of the neurochemical imbalances and pathophysiological mechanisms underlying various conditions. Medications are carefully prescribed and monitored by healthcare professionals to ensure efficacy and minimize adverse effects.

Categories of Pharmacological Interventions

1. **Antidepressants**: These medications are primarily used to treat depression but are also effective for anxiety disorders, obsessive-compulsive disorder (OCD), and certain chronic pain conditions. They work by altering the levels of neurotransmitters in the brain, such as serotonin, norepinephrine, and dopamine.

   - **Selective Serotonin Reuptake Inhibitors (SSRIs)**: SSRIs, such as fluoxetine and sertraline, increase serotonin levels in the brain by inhibiting its reuptake into neurons. They are the first-line treatment for depression and anxiety due to their favorable side effect profile.

- **Serotonin-Norepinephrine Reuptake Inhibitors (SNRIs)**: SNRIs, like venlafaxine and duloxetine, increase levels of both serotonin and norepinephrine. They are used for major depressive disorder, generalized anxiety disorder, and neuropathic pain.
- **Tricyclic Antidepressants (TCAs)**: Older antidepressants such as amitriptyline and nortriptyline are effective but have more side effects, including weight gain, dry mouth, and dizziness. They are sometimes used for treatment-resistant depression and chronic pain conditions.
- **Monoamine Oxidase Inhibitors (MAOIs)**: MAOIs, such as phenelzine, are effective but rarely used due to severe dietary restrictions and potential side effects. They are reserved for treatment-resistant depression.

2. **Antipsychotics**: These medications are used to treat schizophrenia, bipolar disorder, and severe depression. They help manage symptoms such as hallucinations, delusions, and disorganized thinking.

   - **Typical Antipsychotics**: Also known as first-generation antipsychotics, such as haloperidol and chlorpromazine, these medications primarily block dopamine receptors. They are effective but can cause significant side effects, including extrapyramidal symptoms (EPS) like tardive dyskinesia.
   - **Atypical Antipsychotics**: Second-generation antipsychotics, such as risperidone, olanzapine, and aripiprazole, target both

dopamine and serotonin receptors. They have a lower risk of EPS but can cause metabolic side effects like weight gain and diabetes.

3. **Anxiolytics and Sedatives**: These medications are used to treat anxiety disorders, insomnia, and other conditions requiring sedation.

   - **Benzodiazepines**: Drugs like diazepam and lorazepam enhance the neurotransmitter gamma-aminobutyric acid (GABA) effect. They are effective for short-term relief of severe anxiety but carry risks of dependence and withdrawal.
   - **Non-Benzodiazepine Sedatives**: Medications such as zolpidem and eszopiclone are used for insomnia. They have a lower risk of dependence compared to benzodiazepines but still require careful monitoring.

4. **Mood Stabilizers**: Used primarily for bipolar disorder, these medications help stabilize mood swings and prevent manic and depressive episodes.

   - **Lithium**: A classic mood stabilizer, lithium is highly effective but requires regular blood monitoring due to its narrow therapeutic range and potential for toxicity.
   - **Anticonvulsants**: Medications like valproate, lamotrigine, and carbamazepine are also used as mood stabilizers. They help manage both manic and depressive episodes and are often used in patients who do not tolerate lithium.

5. **Stimulants and Non-Stimulant Medications for ADHD**: These medications are used to treat attention-deficit/hyperactivity disorder (ADHD) by increasing attention and reducing hyperactive and impulsive behaviors.

   - **Stimulants**: Drugs like methylphenidate and amphetamine salts increase dopamine and norepinephrine levels in the brain. They are the most effective treatment for ADHD but have potential side effects such as increased heart rate and appetite suppression.
   - **Non-Stimulants**: Medications such as atomoxetine and guanfacine are alternatives for patients who cannot tolerate stimulants. They are generally less effective but have a different side effect profile.

6. **Antiepileptic Drugs (AEDs)**: Used primarily to treat epilepsy, these medications can also be effective in mood stabilization and the management of neuropathic pain.

   - **Common AEDs**: Medications like phenytoin, levetiracetam, and lamotrigine stabilize neuronal membranes and reduce excessive neuronal firing. They require careful dosing and monitoring for potential side effects and interactions.

Considerations and Monitoring

1. **Personalized Medicine**: The choice of pharmacological intervention is highly individualized, considering the patient's

specific diagnosis, symptom profile, comorbid conditions, and potential for side effects. Genetic testing and biomarkers are increasingly used to tailor treatments to individual patients.

2. **Side Effects and Management**: Monitoring for side effects is crucial in pharmacological treatment. Common side effects range from mild (e.g., gastrointestinal upset, headache) to severe (e.g., metabolic syndrome, EPS). Regular follow-up appointments are necessary to adjust dosages and manage adverse effects.

3. **Compliance and Adherence**: Ensuring that patients adhere to their medication regimen is a significant challenge. Strategies to improve adherence include patient education, simplifying medication regimens, and addressing barriers to compliance such as forgetfulness or misunderstanding of the treatment plan.

4. **Polypharmacy**: Many patients, particularly those with complex conditions, maybe on multiple medications. Polypharmacy increases the risk of drug interactions and side effects, necessitating careful management and regular review of all medications a patient is taking.

In conclusion, pharmacological interventions play a vital role in the management of neurological and psychiatric disorders. By carefully selecting and monitoring medications, healthcare providers can significantly improve patient outcomes, helping individuals manage their symptoms and achieve a better quality of life. Advances in personalized medicine and ongoing research continue to refine these interventions, offering hope for more effective and targeted treatments in the future.

7.4 Emerging Technologies in Neuropsychology: Neurofeedback, Brain Stimulation, and More

Emerging technologies in neuropsychology are revolutionizing the diagnosis and treatment of neurological and psychiatric disorders. These innovative approaches, including neurofeedback, brain stimulation techniques, and other advanced methodologies, offer new avenues for enhancing brain function, promoting neuroplasticity, and improving patient outcomes. This section delves into some of the most promising technologies in neuropsychology and their applications.

Neurofeedback

- **Definition and Mechanism**: Neurofeedback is a type of biofeedback that uses real-time monitoring of brain activity to teach self-regulation of brain function. By providing feedback on brainwave patterns through visual or auditory signals, individuals learn to modify their neural activity to achieve desired mental states.
- **Applications and Benefits**: Neurofeedback is used to treat conditions such as attention-deficit/hyperactivity disorder (ADHD), anxiety, depression, epilepsy, and post-traumatic stress disorder (PTSD). The technique helps improve focus, reduce anxiety, enhance mood, and stabilize neural function. It is non-invasive, with minimal side effects, making it a safe option for a wide range of patients.
- **Process**: During a neurofeedback session, electrodes are placed on the scalp to measure brainwave activity. This activity is displayed on a computer screen, and patients engage in tasks or games that encourage the production of desired brainwave patterns. Over time,

patients learn to regulate their brain activity, leading to improvements in symptoms and overall brain function.

Brain Stimulation Techniques

1. Transcranial Magnetic Stimulation (TMS):

- **Mechanism and Procedure**: TMS uses magnetic fields to stimulate nerve cells in the brain. A coil placed near the scalp generates magnetic pulses that penetrate the skull and induce electrical currents in targeted brain regions.
- **Applications**: TMS is primarily used to treat major depressive disorder, especially in patients who do not respond to traditional treatments. It is also being explored for other conditions such as OCD, PTSD, and chronic pain.
- **Benefits**: TMS is non-invasive and has a favorable side effect profile compared to pharmacological treatments. It has been shown to significantly reduce depressive symptoms and improve mood.

2. Transcranial Direct Current Stimulation (tDCS):

- **Mechanism and Procedure**: tDCS involves the application of a low electrical current to the scalp through electrodes. This current modulates neuronal activity, enhancing or inhibiting brain function in targeted areas.
- **Applications**: tDCS is used to treat depression, anxiety, schizophrenia, and cognitive impairments. It is also used in

cognitive enhancement and rehabilitation after stroke or traumatic brain injury.

- **Benefits**: tDCS is relatively easy to administer, cost-effective, and has minimal side effects. It can enhance cognitive functions such as learning, memory, and executive functioning.

3. Deep Brain Stimulation (DBS):

- **Mechanism and Procedure**: DBS involves the surgical implantation of electrodes into specific brain regions. These electrodes deliver continuous electrical impulses to modulate abnormal brain activity.
- **Applications**: DBS is used to treat movement disorders such as Parkinson's disease, dystonia, and essential tremor. It is also being explored for treatment-resistant depression and OCD.
- **Benefits**: DBS can provide significant symptom relief for patients with severe and treatment-resistant conditions. It allows for adjustable and reversible modulation of brain activity.

Other Emerging Technologies

1. Virtual Reality (VR) and Augmented Reality (AR):

- **Applications**: VR and AR are used for exposure therapy in anxiety disorders, PTSD, and phobias. They create immersive environments where patients can safely confront and manage their fears.

- **Benefits**: These technologies provide controlled and customizable therapeutic experiences, enhancing patient engagement and treatment efficacy.

2. Neuroimaging and Neuromodulation:

- **Applications**: Advanced neuroimaging techniques such as functional MRI (fMRI) and positron emission tomography (PET) provide detailed insights into brain function and connectivity. Neuromodulation techniques, including repetitive TMS (rTMS) and focused ultrasound, offer precise modulation of brain activity.
- **Benefits**: These technologies enhance the understanding of brain disorders, inform treatment planning, and improve the precision of therapeutic interventions.

3. Artificial Intelligence (AI) and Machine Learning:

- **Applications**: AI and machine learning algorithms analyze vast amounts of neuropsychological data to identify patterns, predict outcomes, and personalize treatments. They are used in diagnostic tools, treatment planning, and monitoring patient progress.
- **Benefits**: AI-driven technologies improve diagnostic accuracy, optimize treatment strategies, and provide real-time feedback, enhancing the overall effectiveness of neuropsychological interventions.

In conclusion, emerging technologies in neuropsychology, such as neurofeedback, brain stimulation techniques, VR, neuroimaging, and AI, are transforming the landscape of mental health care. These innovative approaches offer new possibilities for understanding and treating brain disorders, improving patient outcomes, and advancing the field of neuropsychology. As research and development continue, these technologies are expected to become integral components of comprehensive neuropsychological care, offering hope and improved quality of life for individuals with neurological and psychiatric conditions.

Chapter 8: Future Directions in Neuropsychology

The field of neuropsychology is evolving rapidly, with emerging technologies and novel research continuously reshaping our understanding of brain function and mental health. As we look to the future, several key areas hold promise for significant advancements in neuropsychology, including personalized medicine, advancements in neuroimaging, integration of artificial intelligence, and the development of innovative therapeutic approaches. These future directions aim to enhance diagnostic accuracy, treatment efficacy, and overall patient outcomes.

Personalized Medicine

Personalized medicine represents a paradigm shift in neuropsychology, moving away from a one-size-fits-all approach to tailored treatments based on an individual's unique genetic, neurobiological, and psychological profile. Advances in genomics and biomarker research are facilitating this transition. By identifying genetic markers and neurobiological signatures associated with specific disorders, clinicians can develop more precise diagnostic tools and customize treatment plans. Personalized medicine aims to optimize therapeutic interventions, minimize side effects, and improve overall treatment efficacy, leading to better patient outcomes and more efficient healthcare delivery.

Advancements in Neuroimaging

Neuroimaging technologies are continually advancing, providing deeper insights into brain structure and function. Techniques such as functional magnetic resonance imaging (fMRI), positron emission tomography (PET), and diffusion tensor imaging (DTI) are becoming more sophisticated, offering higher resolution and more detailed images of brain activity and connectivity. These advancements are enhancing our understanding of the neural mechanisms underlying cognitive and emotional processes and the pathophysiology of various neuropsychological disorders. Future developments may include real-time neuroimaging, enabling dynamic monitoring of brain activity during cognitive tasks or therapeutic interventions. This could revolutionize both diagnostic practices and treatment monitoring, allowing for more precise and adaptive clinical approaches.

Integration of Artificial Intelligence

Artificial intelligence (AI) and machine learning are poised to transform neuropsychology by analyzing vast amounts of data to identify patterns and predict outcomes. AI algorithms can process complex datasets, including neuroimaging scans, genetic information, and clinical records, to uncover subtle correlations that may be missed by human analysts. In the future, AI-driven tools could assist in early diagnosis, personalized treatment planning, and ongoing monitoring of patient progress. For example, AI could predict the risk of developing certain disorders based on genetic and neuroimaging data or recommend personalized interventions based on individual response patterns. The integration of AI into neuropsychology promises to enhance diagnostic accuracy, optimize treatment strategies, and improve patient outcomes.

Innovative Therapeutic Approaches

The development of new therapeutic approaches is a key focus in the future of neuropsychology. Neurostimulation techniques, such as transcranial magnetic stimulation (TMS) and deep brain stimulation (DBS), are being refined and expanded for a wider range of disorders. These techniques offer non-invasive or minimally invasive options for modulating brain activity and alleviating symptoms. Additionally, neurofeedback and virtual reality (VR) therapies are gaining traction as effective treatments for various conditions, including anxiety, PTSD, and cognitive impairments. Future research may explore combining these modalities with pharmacological interventions or traditional psychotherapy to enhance their efficacy. The continued exploration of these innovative therapies holds great promise for improving mental health care.

Ethical and Societal Considerations

As neuropsychology advances, it is crucial to address ethical and societal considerations. The use of genetic information and AI in diagnosis and treatment planning raises concerns about privacy, consent, and potential biases in data interpretation. Ensuring equitable access to advanced neuropsychological interventions and preventing disparities in care will be essential. Additionally, the long-term effects of emerging therapies, particularly neurostimulation and neurofeedback, need thorough investigation to ensure safety and efficacy. Ongoing dialogue among researchers, clinicians, ethicists, and policymakers will be vital to navigate these challenges and promote responsible advancements in the field.

Collaborative and Interdisciplinary Research

Future advancements in neuropsychology will likely stem from collaborative and interdisciplinary research efforts. Integrating insights from neuroscience, psychology, genetics, computer science, and engineering can foster innovative approaches to understanding and treating brain disorders. Collaborative research networks and data-sharing initiatives can accelerate the discovery of novel biomarkers, therapeutic targets, and intervention strategies. Encouraging interdisciplinary collaboration and knowledge exchange will be crucial for driving the field forward and translating research findings into clinical practice.

In conclusion, the future of neuropsychology is marked by exciting possibilities for personalized medicine, advanced neuroimaging, AI integration, and innovative therapies. These developments hold the potential to transform diagnostic and therapeutic practices, ultimately improving patient outcomes and enhancing our understanding of brain function and mental health. However, addressing ethical considerations and promoting interdisciplinary collaboration will be essential to realizing these advancements responsibly and equitably. As the field continues to evolve, neuropsychology will play an increasingly vital role in advancing mental health care and improving the lives of individuals with neurological and psychiatric disorders.

8.1 Advances in Neuroimaging and Brain Mapping

Advances in neuroimaging and brain mapping are at the forefront of neuropsychological research, providing unprecedented insights into the structure and function of the brain. These technologies have revolutionized our understanding of neural processes, enabling precise mapping of brain activity and connectivity. With continuous innovations, neuroimaging is becoming increasingly sophisticated, enhancing our ability to diagnose and treat neurological and psychiatric disorders.

Functional Magnetic Resonance Imaging (fMRI)

Functional Magnetic Resonance Imaging (fMRI) measures brain activity by detecting changes in blood flow. This technique leverages the fact that cerebral blood flow and neuronal activation are closely linked. When a brain region is more active, it receives more blood. fMRI captures these changes, providing real-time images of brain activity. It has become a cornerstone of cognitive neuroscience, helping researchers identify brain regions associated with specific cognitive functions, such as memory, attention, and language. Future advances in fMRI may include higher spatial and temporal resolution, allowing for more detailed and accurate mapping of brain activity.

Positron Emission Tomography (PET)

Positron Emission Tomography (PET) involves injecting a radioactive tracer into the bloodstream. This tracer binds to specific molecules in the brain, allowing researchers to visualize and measure biological processes such as glucose metabolism, neurotransmitter activity, and receptor binding. PET is particularly valuable for studying the pathophysiology of neurodegenerative diseases like Alzheimer's and Parkinson's. Innovations in PET imaging, including the development of new tracers, are enhancing its ability to detect early changes in brain function and monitor disease progression.

Diffusion Tensor Imaging (DTI)

Diffusion Tensor Imaging (DTI) is a type of MRI that maps the diffusion of water molecules in brain tissue. It provides detailed images of white matter tracts, the pathways that connect different brain regions. DTI is crucial for understanding brain connectivity and how disruptions in these networks contribute to various neurological and psychiatric disorders. Advances in DTI technology are improving our ability to visualize complex neural networks and study their role in cognitive and emotional processes. Enhanced resolution and data analysis techniques are helping researchers uncover the intricate wiring of the brain and its implications for health and disease.

Magnetoencephalography (MEG)

Magnetoencephalography (MEG) measures the magnetic fields produced by neuronal activity. It offers excellent temporal resolution, capturing brain activity on the order of milliseconds. MEG is particularly useful for studying the dynamics of neural networks and how they change during different cognitive tasks. It is also used in pre-surgical mapping to identify critical brain areas that need to be preserved during surgery. Future developments in MEG technology aim to improve its spatial resolution and make it more accessible for clinical use.

Near-Infrared Spectroscopy (NIRS)

Near-infrared spectroscopy (NIRS) is a non-invasive technique that uses near-infrared light to measure brain activity. It is portable and relatively low-cost compared to other neuroimaging methods, making it suitable for various clinical and research settings. NIRS is particularly useful for studying brain function in infants and young children, populations that are challenging to assess with other neuroimaging techniques. Advances in NIRS technology are focusing on improving signal quality and expanding its applications in cognitive and clinical neuroscience.

Brain Mapping and Connectomics

Brain mapping involves creating detailed maps of brain structure and function. Connectomics is a related field that aims to map the brain's entire network of connections, known as the connectome. Advances in both areas are driven by the development of high-resolution imaging techniques and powerful computational tools. These advances are providing deeper insights into how different brain regions interact and how disruptions in these networks contribute to disease. Large-scale projects like the Human Connectome Project are creating comprehensive maps of the brain's connectivity, offering valuable resources for researchers worldwide.

Integration of Multimodal Imaging

Combining data from different neuroimaging modalities, known as multimodal imaging, is a powerful approach to studying the brain. For example, integrating fMRI and DTI data can provide complementary information about brain function and connectivity. Advances in data integration techniques are enhancing our ability to understand complex brain processes and their relationship to behavior and disease. This holistic approach is helping researchers develop more comprehensive models of brain function and improve diagnostic and therapeutic strategies.

Artificial Intelligence and Machine Learning

Artificial Intelligence (AI) and machine learning are transforming neuroimaging by enabling the analysis of large and complex datasets. These technologies can identify patterns and relationships that are not apparent to human observers, leading to discoveries about brain function and disease mechanisms. AI is also improving the accuracy and efficiency of image processing and analysis, making it possible to extract more information from neuroimaging data. Future developments in AI and machine learning are expected to further enhance the capabilities of neuroimaging and brain mapping.

In conclusion, advances in neuroimaging and brain mapping are significantly enhancing our understanding of the brain. These technologies provide detailed insights into brain structure and function, improving diagnostic accuracy, and guiding the development of new treatments. As innovations continue to emerge, the field of neuropsychology will benefit from more precise and comprehensive tools for studying the brain and addressing neurological and psychiatric disorders.

8.2 The Role of Genetics and Epigenetics in Neuropsychology

The role of genetics and epigenetics in neuropsychology is increasingly recognized as crucial for understanding the development, function, and disorders of the brain. These fields explore how genetic variations and modifications in gene expression influence neural processes and behaviors, providing insights into the biological underpinnings of cognitive functions and mental health conditions. This section delves into the contributions of genetics and epigenetics to neuropsychology, highlighting their implications for the diagnosis, treatment, and prevention of neurological and psychiatric disorders.

Genetics in Neuropsychology

Genetic Variability and Brain Function: Genetic variability refers to the differences in DNA sequences among individuals, which can affect brain structure and function. Specific genes are linked to various aspects of neural development and functioning, including synaptic transmission, neurogenesis, and brain plasticity. For instance, genes related to neurotransmitter systems, such as the serotonin transporter gene (5-HTTLPR) and the dopamine receptor gene (DRD4), have been implicated in mood regulation, impulsivity, and cognitive functions. Variations in these genes can influence susceptibility to disorders such as depression, ADHD, and schizophrenia.

Genetic Disorders and Cognitive Impairments: Certain genetic mutations or chromosomal abnormalities can lead to neurodevelopmental and neurodegenerative disorders. Conditions like Down syndrome, Fragile X syndrome, and Huntington's disease are caused by specific genetic alterations and are associated with distinct cognitive and behavioral profiles. Understanding the genetic basis of these disorders aids in early diagnosis, targeted interventions, and the development of gene-based therapies. Research in this area continues to uncover new genetic risk factors for a wide range of neuropsychological conditions.

Genome-Wide Association Studies (GWAS): GWAS are large-scale studies that identify genetic variations associated with specific traits or disorders. By scanning the genomes of many individuals, researchers can pinpoint common genetic markers linked to neuropsychological conditions. These studies have identified numerous loci associated with psychiatric disorders, such as autism spectrum disorder, bipolar disorder, and schizophrenia. GWAS provides valuable insights into the complex genetic architecture of these conditions, highlighting potential targets for therapeutic intervention.

Epigenetics in Neuropsychology

Epigenetic Mechanisms: Epigenetics involves the study of heritable changes in gene expression that do not involve alterations in the DNA sequence. Key epigenetic mechanisms include DNA methylation, histone modification, and non-coding RNA activity. These processes regulate gene activity in response to environmental factors, thereby influencing brain development and function. Epigenetic changes can be triggered by various factors, including stress, diet, toxins, and social experiences, making them a crucial link between the environment and genetic expression.

Impact on Brain Development and Plasticity: Epigenetic modifications play a vital role in brain development and plasticity, the brain's ability to reorganize and adapt throughout life. For example, early-life stress can lead to long-lasting epigenetic changes that affect stress-response genes and increase vulnerability to mental health disorders. Conversely, positive experiences, such as enriched environments and learning opportunities, can promote beneficial epigenetic modifications that enhance cognitive functions and resilience. Understanding these dynamics offers pathways for developing interventions that promote optimal brain health.

Epigenetics and Mental Health: Epigenetic changes are implicated in the pathophysiology of various psychiatric disorders. For instance, alterations in DNA methylation patterns have been observed in individuals with depression, PTSD, and schizophrenia. These changes can affect genes involved in neurotransmitter regulation, neuroplasticity, and immune responses, contributing to the onset and progression of mental health conditions. Epigenetic research is advancing our understanding of how life experiences interact with genetic predispositions to influence mental health, paving the way for personalized therapeutic approaches.

Therapeutic Implications: The study of epigenetics has significant therapeutic implications for neuropsychology. Epigenetic modifications are potentially reversible, making them attractive targets for novel treatments. Epigenetic therapies, such as histone deacetylase inhibitors and DNA methyltransferase inhibitors, are being explored for their potential to modulate gene expression and alleviate symptoms of neuropsychological disorders. Additionally, lifestyle interventions, including diet, exercise, and stress management, can induce beneficial epigenetic changes, offering non-pharmacological strategies for promoting mental health.

Future Directions

- **Integrating Genetics and Epigenetics**: Future research in neuropsychology is likely to focus on the integration of genetic and epigenetic data to provide a comprehensive understanding of brain function and disorders. Combining genetic susceptibility with epigenetic modifications will offer deeper insights into individual differences in cognition, behavior, and mental health. This integrative approach can lead to the development of more precise diagnostic tools and personalized treatment strategies.
- **Ethical Considerations**: As research in genetics and epigenetics progresses, ethical considerations will become increasingly important. Issues related to genetic privacy, informed consent, and the potential for genetic discrimination need careful attention. Ensuring that advances in this field are applied ethically and equitably will be crucial for maximizing their benefits and minimizing potential harms.

In conclusion, genetics and epigenetics play pivotal roles in neuropsychology, offering valuable insights into the biological basis of brain function and mental health. Advances in these fields are enhancing our ability to diagnose, treat, and prevent neuropsychological disorders, paving the way for personalized and effective interventions. As research continues to evolve, the integration of genetic and epigenetic knowledge will be essential for advancing our understanding of the complex interplay between genes, environment, and brain health.

8.3 Ethical Considerations in Neuropsychological Research and Practice

Ethical considerations in neuropsychological research and practice are paramount, given the sensitive nature of studying and treating brain function and behavior. These considerations span informed consent, confidentiality, data management, and the implications of findings for individuals and society. Upholding ethical standards ensures that research and clinical practices respect participants' rights and welfare while advancing scientific knowledge and therapeutic interventions.

Informed Consent

Informed consent is a foundational ethical principle in neuropsychological research and practice. Participants must be fully informed about the study's purpose, procedures, risks, and benefits before agreeing to participate. This process involves clear communication and ensuring that individuals understand what their involvement entails. Special attention is required when dealing with vulnerable populations, such as children, individuals with cognitive impairments, or psychiatric conditions. Researchers and clinicians must ensure that consent is obtained freely, without coercion, and that participants can withdraw at any time without penalty.

Confidentiality and Privacy

Maintaining confidentiality and privacy is crucial in neuropsychology. Researchers and clinicians handle sensitive data, including cognitive assessments, neuroimaging results, and personal histories. Protecting this information from unauthorized access and ensuring its use is restricted to the stated purposes are ethical imperatives. Anonymizing data, using secure storage methods, and adhering to legal and institutional guidelines are essential practices. Breaches of confidentiality can harm participants, erode trust, and compromise the integrity of research and clinical practice.

Data Management

Ethical data management involves responsibly collecting, storing, and sharing data. Researchers must ensure the accuracy and integrity of their data, avoiding practices such as data fabrication, falsification, and selective reporting. Sharing data with the scientific community can promote transparency and reproducibility but must be balanced with protecting participants' confidentiality. Establishing data-sharing agreements that outline the terms and conditions for access and use is critical. Ethical data management also includes the appropriate handling of incidental findings, which are unexpected results that may have clinical significance for participants.

Neuroimaging and Genetic Data

The use of neuroimaging and genetic data in neuropsychology raises specific ethical issues. These data types can reveal detailed information about an individual's brain structure, function, and genetic predispositions, potentially impacting their identity and privacy. Informed consent processes must address the implications of these findings, including the potential for discovering incidental results that could affect the participant's health or psychological well-being. Researchers and clinicians must navigate the ethical complexities of reporting such findings and the potential for psychological harm or anxiety.

Ethical Implications of Findings

The findings from neuropsychological research can have far-reaching implications for individuals and society. Discoveries about the biological basis of behavior and mental health conditions can influence public perceptions, policy decisions, and clinical practices. Researchers and clinicians must communicate their findings responsibly, avoiding overgeneralizations and ensuring that the limitations and context of the research are clear. Misinterpretation or misapplication of neuropsychological findings can lead to stigma, discrimination, and unwarranted changes in public policy or clinical practice.

Dual-Use Concerns

Neuropsychological research can have dual-use potential, meaning it can be used for beneficial or harmful purposes. For example, insights into brain function can enhance treatments for neurological disorders but could also be used to develop techniques for manipulating behavior or cognition. Researchers must be aware of the dual-use potential of their work and take steps to mitigate the risks of misuse. This involves adhering to ethical guidelines, engaging in open dialogue about the potential applications of their research, and advocating for policies that prevent misuse.

Equity and Access

Ethical practice in neuropsychology includes promoting equity and access to research participation and clinical interventions. Efforts should be made to include diverse populations in research studies to ensure that findings are generalizable and applicable to different groups. Clinicians should strive to provide equitable access to neuropsychological assessments and treatments, addressing barriers such as socioeconomic status, geographic location, and cultural differences. Ensuring that advancements in neuropsychology benefit all segments of society is a critical ethical concern.

Professional Competence and Integrity

Maintaining professional competence and integrity is essential in neuropsychological research and practice. Researchers and clinicians must engage in ongoing education and training to stay current with advancements in the field. They should adhere to established ethical guidelines and professional standards, avoiding conflicts of interest and ensuring that their work is guided by scientific rigor and ethical principles. Peer review, collaboration, and accountability are important mechanisms for upholding professional integrity and advancing the field responsibly.

In conclusion, ethical considerations in neuropsychological research and practice are multifaceted and vital for protecting participants' rights and well-being. Upholding principles of informed consent, confidentiality, data management, and responsible communication ensures that neuropsychological research and interventions are conducted with integrity and respect for individuals and society. As the field continues to advance, ongoing attention to ethical issues will be essential for promoting trust, advancing knowledge, and improving mental health care.

8.4 The Future of Neuropsychology: Integrating Neuroscience, Psychology, and Technology

The future of neuropsychology lies in the seamless integration of neuroscience, psychology, and technology. This multidisciplinary approach promises to deepen our understanding of brain-behavior relationships, enhance diagnostic precision, and revolutionize therapeutic interventions. As advancements in each field converge, neuropsychology is poised to transform how we study, diagnose, and treat cognitive and emotional disorders.

Neuroscience and Neuropsychology Integration

Neuroscience provides the biological foundation for neuropsychology, offering insights into the neural mechanisms underlying cognitive functions and behaviors. Advances in neuroimaging techniques, such as functional MRI (fMRI), positron emission tomography (PET), and magnetoencephalography (MEG), allow for detailed visualization of brain activity and connectivity. These tools enable neuropsychologists to correlate specific brain regions with cognitive processes and behavioral outcomes, enhancing our understanding of disorders like schizophrenia, autism, and ADHD.

Neuropsychologists increasingly leverage neuroscience to develop more accurate models of brain function. For instance, research on neural networks and brain plasticity informs our understanding of how the brain adapts following injury or disease. This knowledge is critical for developing effective rehabilitation strategies and cognitive training programs aimed at harnessing the brain's capacity for reorganization and recovery.

Psychological Insights

Psychology contributes to neuropsychology by providing a framework for understanding behavior and mental processes. Cognitive psychology, in particular, offers theories and models that describe how we perceive, think, learn, and remember. Integrating these psychological theories with neuroscientific data allows for a more comprehensive understanding of cognitive functions.

Clinical psychology plays a vital role in neuropsychological assessment and intervention. Psychological principles guide the development of assessment tools that measure cognitive abilities, emotional functioning, and behavior. These tools are essential for diagnosing conditions such as dementia, traumatic brain injury, and developmental disorders. Additionally, psychological therapies, such as cognitive-behavioral therapy (CBT), are informed by neuropsychological research, allowing for evidence-based approaches to treatment.

Technological Innovations

Technological advancements are driving the future of neuropsychology, offering new tools and methods for research and practice. Artificial intelligence (AI) and machine learning are particularly transformative, enabling the analysis of complex neuroimaging and genetic data. These technologies can identify patterns and biomarkers associated with specific disorders, leading to more precise diagnoses and personalized treatment plans.

Virtual reality (VR) and augmented reality (AR) are emerging as powerful tools for neuropsychological assessment and rehabilitation. VR environments can simulate real-world tasks, providing an immersive platform for evaluating cognitive functions and social behaviors. Similarly, AR applications can enhance cognitive training and therapeutic exercises by integrating interactive digital elements into the physical world.

Neurofeedback and brain-computer interfaces (BCIs) represent another frontier in neuropsychological intervention. These technologies allow individuals to receive real-time feedback on their brain activity and learn to modulate it to improve cognitive and emotional functioning. BCIs, in particular, hold promise for individuals with severe motor impairments, enabling communication and control through direct brain signals.

Future Directions

The future of neuropsychology will likely see greater emphasis on personalized and precision medicine. Integrating genetic, epigenetic, and neuroimaging data will enable neuropsychologists to develop individualized profiles of brain function and risk factors. This personalized approach will facilitate targeted interventions that are tailored to the unique needs and characteristics of each individual.

Collaborative research across disciplines will be essential for advancing neuropsychology. Partnerships between neuroscientists, psychologists, computer scientists, and clinicians will foster innovative approaches to understanding and treating cognitive and emotional disorders.

Interdisciplinary training programs will prepare the next generation of neuropsychologists to navigate the complexities of this integrated field.

Ethical considerations will remain paramount as technology advances. Ensuring informed consent, protecting privacy, and addressing potential biases in AI algorithms will be critical for maintaining the integrity and trustworthiness of neuropsychological research and practice.

In conclusion, the future of neuropsychology lies in the integration of neuroscience, psychology, and technology. This multidisciplinary approach will enhance our understanding of the brain and its functions, leading to more precise diagnoses and effective interventions. As these fields continue to converge, neuropsychology will play a pivotal role in improving mental health care and promoting cognitive and emotional well-being.

Conclusion

In conclusion, the journey through the intricate landscape of neuropsychology reveals a profound understanding of the complex connections between brain function and the science behind behavior, cognition, and emotion. This field, positioned at the intersection of neuroscience and psychology, offers a comprehensive framework for exploring how neural mechanisms translate into the diverse spectrum of human experiences.

Bridging Neuroscience and Psychology

Neuropsychology stands as a bridge between the biological underpinnings of brain activity and the psychological manifestations of behavior and thought. By integrating insights from neuroscience, neuropsychologists uncover the structural and functional dynamics of the brain, mapping out regions and networks that contribute to cognitive processes and emotional states. This integration allows for a more holistic understanding of the mind, moving beyond isolated perspectives to embrace the complexity of human functioning.

Advancements in Understanding Brain Function

The advancements in neuroimaging and brain mapping technologies have revolutionized our ability to visualize and comprehend brain activity. Techniques such as fMRI, PET, and MEG have provided unprecedented insights into the brain's inner workings, enabling researchers to pinpoint areas associated with specific cognitive functions and behaviors. These tools have not only deepened our understanding of healthy brain function but have also illuminated the neural correlates of various neurological and psychiatric disorders, paving the way for more accurate diagnoses and targeted treatments.

Genetic and Epigenetic Contributions

The exploration of genetic and epigenetic factors has further enriched our understanding of brain function and its impact on behavior and cognition. Genetic studies have identified numerous genes associated with cognitive abilities and mental health conditions, highlighting the heritable nature of these traits. Meanwhile, epigenetic research has demonstrated how environmental influences can alter gene expression, emphasizing the dynamic interplay between genes and the environment. This knowledge underscores the importance of considering both genetic predispositions and life experiences in understanding individual differences in cognitive and emotional functioning.

Ethical Considerations and Future Directions

The ethical considerations inherent in neuropsychological research and practice cannot be overstated. Ensuring informed consent, protecting confidentiality, and addressing potential biases are paramount to conducting responsible and respectful research. As the field advances, ongoing attention to ethical issues will be crucial for maintaining public trust and safeguarding the rights of research participants.

Looking ahead, the future of neuropsychology promises exciting possibilities. The integration of neuroscience, psychology, and technology will continue to drive innovation, leading to more personalized and effective interventions. Emerging technologies such as AI, VR, and BCIs hold immense potential for enhancing diagnostic precision and therapeutic outcomes. Collaborative efforts across disciplines will foster a deeper understanding of the brain and its functions, ultimately improving mental health care and promoting cognitive and emotional well-being.

Impact on Mental Health and Society

The implications of neuropsychological research extend beyond the realm of science, influencing clinical practice, education, and public policy. By elucidating the neural basis of cognitive and emotional processes, neuropsychology informs the development of evidence-based interventions for a wide range of conditions, from developmental disorders to neurodegenerative diseases. This knowledge empowers clinicians to provide more effective treatments, educators to design better learning environments, and policymakers to create informed health strategies.

Moreover, neuropsychology's contributions to understanding the brain have profound societal implications. As we gain insights into the neural mechanisms underlying behavior and cognition, we can challenge misconceptions, reduce stigma, and foster a more inclusive and compassionate society. The knowledge generated by neuropsychological research has the power to shape public attitudes toward mental health, promoting greater acceptance and support for individuals with cognitive and emotional differences.

A Comprehensive Understanding of the Mind

In sum, neuropsychology offers a comprehensive and nuanced understanding of the mind, grounded in the interplay between brain function and behavior. By integrating insights from neuroscience, psychology, and genetics, this field provides a rich tapestry of knowledge that enhances our comprehension of cognitive processes and emotional states. As we continue to explore the complexities of the brain, neuropsychology will remain at the forefront of efforts to unlock the mysteries of the human mind, ultimately contributing to the betterment of individual lives and society as a whole.

Through this exploration, we come to appreciate the intricate beauty of the brain and its profound impact on who we are. Neuropsychology not only deepens our scientific knowledge but also enriches our understanding of the human experience, offering pathways to enhance mental health and well-being for all.